50 BIBLE TRUTHS ON WEALTH

BY GINO LEITO

Gino Leito is a very skilled teacher in the Kingdom of God. A man anointed to discover keys in the word of God that lead to a victorious life. By grasping the truths and applying the principles noted in this book, we as body of Christ will move forward as we discover the very significant things God says about the topic of wealth. I believe there will be a great transfer of wealth to the children of the Kingdom as the Bible also indicates.

The time has come to destroy the spirit of poverty. There is often a wrong view of money in the kingdom of God. In the past, Satan has made considerable abuse of the ignorance of the church. Remember that God says that His people perish for lack of knowledge (Hosea 4:6). Many Christians saw it as a sin to be rich. Now the time has come for God to get His church out of poverty to rule in the spiritual world of finance.

The kingdom of God is built on the pillars of justice and righteousness. God is looking forward to grant to His children justice and righteousness. Children who believe that they have suffered injustice take hold of the riches in the Kingdom as violent ones. To build the Kingdom by planting churches, schools and accommodations, finances are needed.

The special thing about this book is that it deals with practical lessons about wealth, but at the same time it also explains how to give to God. The giver will be incredibly blessed and protected according to the word of God (Malachi 3:10-11).

- Apostle Oswald Hart

Founder and Visionary of De Rots Amsterdam

** Apostle Oswald leads De Rots Amsterdam, a vibrant Pentecostal church in the city of Amsterdam in the Netherlands. He is a strong apostolic leader with a passionate heart for souls. In his vision it is important that believers reach their spiritual destiny but also their destiny in society. He has made his life goal to change followers into leaders and leaders into agents of change.*

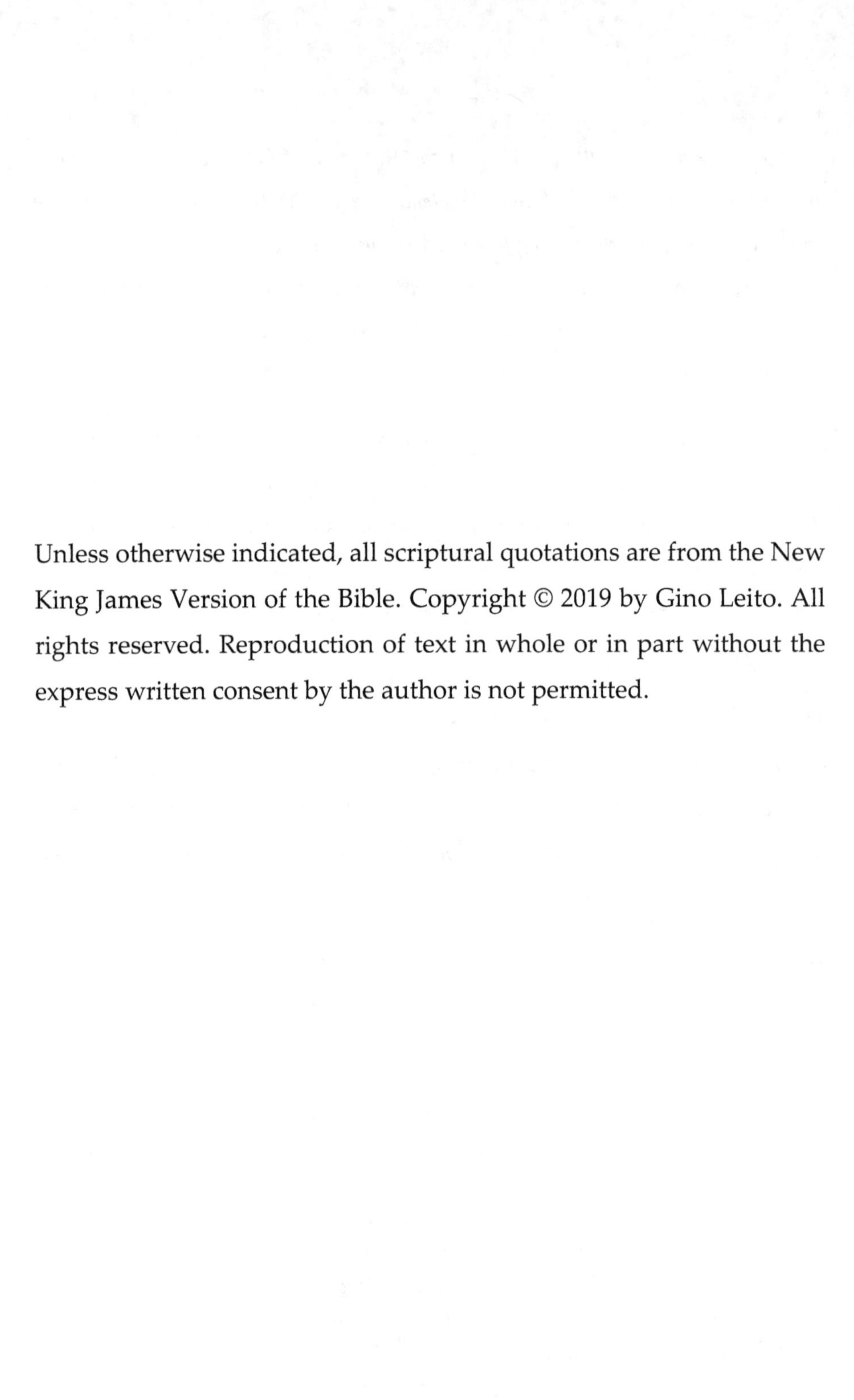

Table of Contents

Introduction 50 Bible Truths on Wealth

The topic of wealth and prosperity is a highly debated topic within the church. Even outside the church walls this topic has gotten attention, which was mainly negative. What's true and what's false? Only the inspired Word of God can give us the correct answer.

In essence, this book will cover 50 simple truths on wealth and prosperity from the Bible. God has pressed upon my heart to study this matter. The main focus of this book is on material wealth and material prosperity. This book does not only offer texts that provide a one-sided and happily ever after fairytale (false) perspective but it'll also provide you with simple practical truths, points for attention and precautions on money, wealth, possessions and prosperity.

It is my heart's greatest desire that this book equips you with more insight and wisdom on this subject.

My prayer is that God, our Father of glory, may give unto you the spirit of wisdom and revelation in the knowledge of Him and His Word. May the eyes of your understanding be enlightened (Ephesians 1:17-18).

Enjoy the read and may you grasp and apply the truths after reading this book!

1. God's Prosperity is All-Inclusive

According to the Merriam-Webster dictionary prosperity is: the condition of being successful or thriving (especially: economic well-being)

The Hebrew word for "to prosper" or "prosperity" in the Old Testament is *tsalach* meaning to rush, to push forward, to break out, come mightily, go over, be good, be meet, be profitable, cause to, effect.

In other English Bible translations than the King James Version *tsalach* and its forms are often translated as to be successful, to succeed and to excel.

> *And the LORD was with Joseph, and he was a **prosperous man**; and he was in the house of his master the Egyptian.*
>
> *And his master saw that the Lord was with him, and that the Lord made all that he did to prosper in his hand.*
>
> Genesis 39:2-3

We know the story of Joseph. Sold as a slave by his jealous brothers he ends up serving the ruler of Egypt, far away from his family and loved ones. However, the Lord still makes everything to succeed in Joseph's hands. Joseph's Egyptian master makes Joseph to be an overseer in his house and the Lord blesses everything the Egyptian had in his house and his field because of Joseph.

So the *"tsalach* prosperity" of Joseph was all-inclusive. God prospered his work so he was successful and this also led to material well-being! Even a golden chain was granted to Joseph (Genesis 41:42). Now I'm not suggesting that every prosperous Christian should own a golden chain that would make the average rapper jealous, but it sure was a clear sign of God's all-inclusive prosperity!

In the New Testament, the Greek word *euodoo* is used for "to prosper". *Euodoo* literally means to grant a prosperous and expeditious journey, to lead by a direct and easy way, to grant a successful issue, to cause to prosper.

> *"Beloved, I wish above all things that thou mayest prosper and be in health, even as thy soul prospereth."*

> *3 John 2*

So what does that mean *even as your soul prospereth*? The Apostle John wrote this letter to his beloved friend Gaius with the intention to encourage him to support the traveling evangelists that spread the Gospel of Truth. Some argue that it was just a general greeting.

I believe that the Apostle John meant to wish his beloved friend well in every sense. The Amplified Bible translation beautifully depicts this:

physically *and* spiritually. In other words, the blessing is directed to his outward and inward being. Besides the physical and spiritual part, the word "prosper" is used which, definition wise, has economic well-being and success inherently attached to it. This is made very clear by the same word that's used in 1 Corinthians 16:2:

> *Now concerning the collection for the saints, as I have given orders to the churches of Galatia, so even so do ye: Upon the first day of the week let every one of you lay by him in store, as God hath* **prospered** *him, that there be no gatherings when I come.*
>
> *1 Corinthians 16:1-2 KJV*

So Paul directs the Christian believers in Corinth to lay by him in store (meaning to lay aside) money each week. They had to lay aside (finances) *as God hath prospered them.* So the link between the words "prosper" (*euodoo*) and finances resonates here in this part of Scripture. It can include financial prosperity. Conclusion: in the Old *and* the New Testament we see how God prospered his people and this prosperity was all-inclusive! It did include material-well-being.

2. God Gives Power To Make Wealth

*But thou shalt remember the LORD thy God: for **it is he that giveth thee power to get wealth**, that he may establish his covenant which he sware unto thy fathers, as it is this day.*

Deuteronomy 8:18

God gives the power to make wealth. In other words, God gives us the ability to make wealth.

He gives us all talents and gifts to make wealth. They're for us to use. Now, well, this is just what He said under the covenant in the Old Testament, some might say.

*For you know the grace of our Lord Jesus Christ, that though He was rich, yet for your sakes He became poor, that you through His poverty **might become** rich.*

2 Corinthians 8:9

Paul states essentially the same in the New Testament: through Christ we may become rich. He has given us this opportunity. He does not want us to bring our talents with us to the grave. We know the parable of the talents (Matthew 25:14-30, Luke 19:11-27), in which a man gives his servants talents and leaves the city for a while. What did he expect? He expected them *to do business until he returned*: to increase, and not to put these talents in the ground and sit around passively until he returned.

Do you know what else the parable of the talents tells us? God always gives us everything we need, so we're able to do what he has called us for. He has given us the power and ability. This principle cannot only be applied to wealth but also to gifts and talents, we have received all things to do what we need to do for Him. We have no excuses!

A final warning note here: always remember that it is GOD that gives you wealth, never forget this Bible truth (Deuteronomy 8:17)!

3. Wealth and Prosperity Are Not Irrelevant and Unspiritual

Jesus knew about the relevance of money, wealth and possessions which is probably the main reason he spoke so many times about these vital subjects. We're talking here about the most influential teacher that has ever lived! Of the 37 parables recorded in the Gospel, about 30-40% covered the topic of money, wealth and possessions. For example, Matthew 13:44-50 records three parables that cover the topic of wealth: the Hidden Treasure, Parable of the Pearl and Drawing in the Net.

Whether a fisherman was listening, a banker, a tax collector, a scribe or housewife (whether or not prudent) they all had to deal with money in one way or the other. In fact, money played a big role of importance in their lives. In our modern-day world, this has not changed. Money is still highly relevant in our society and can't be ignored by any one of us.

Jesus sure knew one thing about capturing the attention of his audience. He focused on the right topics to capture the public's attention but this also says something about the relevance of material prosperity.

It's a misconception to think that wealth and prosperity have no place in the Body of Christ and that these are irrelevant and unspiritual topics. Money *is* relevant for matters in the Kingdom of God. For spreading Bibles, spreading teaching material, building orphanages, handing out food to the needy etc., etc. For all these things we need money. Money is relevant.

Although money is important in spreading the Gospel, we should never overestimate its importance in spreading the Gospel or else we would be downplaying the work of the Apostles and early believers. They had the Spirit and not much more and turned the world upside down (Acts 17:6)!

Many know that there's an entire chapter that speaks about love, which is 1 Corinthians 13. 1 Corinthians 13 consists of only 13 verses. But did you realize that in one of the letters to the Corinthians there are even 2 chapters that speak about money? 2 Corinthians 8 and 9 speak entirely about money and consist of 39 verses! Money and possessions are referenced *more than 2000* times in the Bible! More than faith and love for example! Does that mean that money is more important than love and faith? Absolutely not.

The greatest thing is love (1 Corinthians 13:13) but is material prosperity (money, wealth, possessions) relevant? Yes, it sure is. Is material prosperity unspiritual? Wealth and godliness are certainly not incompatible. Remember, all the righteous rich of the Old Testament? Godly *and* wealthy men like Abraham, Joseph and Job? Their examples tell it all.

Don't be fooled, since it's a common lie to believe that wealth and prosperity are irrelevant and unspiritual. Wealth is not irrelevant and unspiritual. However, on the other hand, lacking wealth is not something spiritual or particularly pious. The word of God is very powerful but be careful: the tradition of men (in other words, cultural customs and practices) have the ability to make the word of God powerless (Mark 7:13)! Put aside your colored glasses (the glasses that give you a distorted and biased view) or your "cultural glasses" and read with an open heart what the Bible has to say about wealth. It's crucial to let this all sink in, in the right way, as how we think about wealth is very important in us receiving it. More about our attitude towards wealth in one of the other truths in this book! The truth will set us free.

4. Wealth Should Be Attracted, Not Pursued

But seek first the Kingdom of God and His righteousness, and all these things shall be added to you.

Matthew 6:33

Seek *first* the Kingdom of God. The word *first* here is from the Greek word *protos* meaning foremost, in the first place and firstly in order and importance. In sum, we should prioritize and pursue God's Kingdom and then *all these things* will pursue us. *All these things* will be attracted when not pursued.

The Lord's blessing that makes rich (Proverbs 10:22) is not limited to location. Look at our heroes of faith. Upon receiving missions from God to go to certain places, did they ever wonder *"hmm how much will it cost me?"* Or *"how much will it profit me"*? Never. Did Abraham do that? Or Paul? They knew that God's work is to be prioritized and that his prosperity would follow them anyhow.

Do not pursue money with what you do. Attract money with what you do.

Follow the example of our heroes of faith. Don't make money your goal. Moreover, do what you do that well, that it will attract money. Money *will* then pursue you. Don't mess up the order by putting money in the first place. In line with that we have Matthew 6:33 as our promise of provision. What else, besides prioritizing Gods Kingdom, is one of the things that gets (prosperity) to pursue you? You must be excellent in the things you do. But, I believe you can only become truly accomplished at something you love. Something you are passionate about. People often try to chase just anything where money can be obtained, but without being passionate about something, it is difficult to perform well and to gain wealth. So one of the first steps is: *find out what you love doing.* Then, pursue these things and do them so well that wealth will ultimately follow (Proverbs 22:29).

What are *all these things* mentioned in Matthew 6:33? The Bible says in Matthew 6:31 that Jesus refers to food, drink and clothing. In essence, these are the things we need. Moreover, the Bible also says that *"whoever pursues righteousness and love finds life,* **prosperity** *and honor (Proverbs 21:21 NIV).* So, you will find *prosperity* when you will pursue His Kingdom of righteousness and love. Remember, the key to these benefits: *prioritizing* your pursuit of God and His Kingdom. Say amen!

5. Wealth is Wisdom and Knowledge

How much better to get wisdom than gold!
And to get understanding is to be chosen rather than silver.
Proverbs 16:16

Solomon, the wisest and probably richest king who has ever lived, stated his main reason for writing Proverbs in the opening verses of Proverbs: to foster the transfer of wisdom, knowledge and (principles for) godly living (Proverbs 1:1-4). A beautiful statement is: *in all thy getting get understanding (Proverbs 4:7)*. If you truly cry out for wisdom you'll find it in God and with God (Proverbs 2:4-6).

There lies so much in wisdom, understanding, insight and knowledge. The benefits are worth more than rubies, gold and silver. Godly wisdom, understanding, insight and knowledge are all precious gems on themselves.

The fear of the Lord *is* the beginning of wisdom and the knowledge of Him *is* understanding (Proverbs 9:10). So you cannot enjoy the fullness of wisdom and knowledge without seeking and knowing Him. Fearing

God in itself is prosperity too: it contributes to our overall well-being.

Godly wisdom and understanding are better than gold and silver (Proverbs 16:16). Wisdom and knowledge are wealth in themselves *but* they also *lead to* wealth. The Bible makes it very clear: there is immense wealth *in* wisdom and knowledge *and* wealth *through* wisdom and knowledge.

6. Wealth Through Wisdom and Knowledge

Happy is the man who finds wisdom,
And the man who finds understanding;
For her proceeds are better than the profits of silver,
And her gain than fine gold.
She is more precious than rubies,
And all the things you may desire cannot compare with her.

Length of days is in her right hand,
In her left hand riches and honor
Proverbs 3:13-16

The wise king Solomon who asked for wisdom knew its value: better than the profits of silver, fine gold and rubies. In other words, wisdom is to be preferred rather than riches. *But* in wisdom's left hand riches and honor are held. So, in other words, wisdom and knowledge are wealth itself AND will make you prosper materially as well. The same link is found elsewhere too. For example in Proverbs 24:4:

> *By knowledge the rooms are filled with all precious and pleasant riches.*

Seeking wisdom and understanding is beneficial for our spiritual lives as God's favor rests upon the seeking of these attributes. The blessings are not merely spiritual but also *material*. By knowledge the rooms are filled. With what? *With all precious and pleasant riches.*

An investment in knowledge pays the best interest. -Benjamin Franklin

The man whose face graces the American 100 dollar bill, Benjamin Franklin, had a lot to say about money. He even wrote bestsellers on wealth. According to Franklin, an investment in knowledge pays the best interest.

I would like to add that an investment in wisdom AND knowledge pays the best interest. It could lead to very high interest, in other words to wealth.

> *With your wisdom and your understanding*
> *You have gained riches for yourself,*
> *And gathered gold and silver into your treasuries;*
> *By your great wisdom in trade you have increased your riches,*
> *And your heart is lifted up because of your riches,*

> *Ezekiel 28:4-5*

Godly wisdom and godly knowledge establish a basis for wealth. Wisdom in trade, in other words, business insight, knowledge and savvy will also make you increase riches (Ezekiel 28:4-5). People, in general, are also willing to pay you for your knowledge and insight on several topics. Which topics? Look around you, it seems like there are experts on everything. Dog whispering, aquarium building, food traveling. You name it. Do you see what these examples tell us? People are willing to pay you for your expertise on all sorts of things! Invest your time in something you love and become an expert. This is a key to wealth!

7. God Should Be Acknowledged in Acquiring Wealth

Honor the Lord with your possessions,
And with the firstfruits of all your increase;
Proverbs 3:9

The Bible says that we should honor the Lord with our possessions and with the *firstfruits* of our increase. *Firstfruits* are the first yield of harvest and giving it to the Lord demonstrated the Israelites' obedience, reverence and dependence on God as their provider.

Honoring God with our possessions and firstfruits shows our gratefulness to Him as our source. Gratefulness creates joy in our hearts, one of the reasons that makes it more blessed to give than to receive (Acts 20:35). Do you know what else it does? It activates a great promise:

So your barns will be filled with plenty,
And your vats will overflow with new wine
Proverbs 3:10

For "plenty" the Hebrew word *saba* is used. In other verses is also translated as full or satisfied.

So your barns will be filled *until it is full*. The vats (containers for drinks) will even receive *more* than its maximum amount. That's what overflow means.

We should acknowledge the Lord with our material but also with our mouth and heart. This creates awe and reverence in our hearts for the Lord God Almighty and His wondrous works. We shouldn't take things for granted that the Lord gave us. Acknowledgment and gratitude bring us to a deeper awareness, knowledge and dimension in God.

Even in the simple and small things we should acknowledge Him. This shows our dependence on Him. How much more with our riches? The riches that can easily distract us from depending on God. We express the sincerity of our love when we give to Him.

Do you know what else acknowledgment and gratefulness do? They stop the craving of your soul for more and more wealth. Acknowledge Him as your perfect provider that gives you all you need (Philippians 4:19).

8. *Giving is Sowing*

The generous soul will be made rich,

And he who waters will also be watered himself.

Proverbs 11:25

But this I say: *He who sows sparingly will also reap sparingly, and*

he who sows bountifully will also reap bountifully;

2 Corinthians 9:6

Throughout the Old Testament and in the New Testament as well, a clear principle is laid out: *giving is sowing.* Synonyms for *bountifully* are plentiful, abundant, plenty, generous and richly. Paul clearly states it: *if you sow richly, you will reap richly.* Give and it shall be given unto you, for by your standard of measure it will be measured to you in return (Luke 6:38). But for this principle of sowing and reaping to be effective we need to understand the conditions laid out for us. First, to whom should we give?

Giving to God

To whom should we give? First and foremost to God. We should honor him with our possessions (Proverbs 3:9). In modern times, our gift will probably consist of money. Giving our money to God does not mean that we go out with our euro banknotes or dollar bills to a nice remote place and throw them in the air saying "Here you go, God". No. In the same way, a farmer does not go out throwing seeds on the pavement and expecting crops to grow.

It means that we ought to give our money and gifts to a fruitful ministry in the Kingdom (for example your local church). Paul was in essence also talking about gathering an offering in the Corinthian church for the saints in Jerusalem when he mentioned the practice of sowing.

Giving to the poor and needy

God also encourages us to be generous and kind to others and share with others around us in an unselfish way (Philippians 2:4). God's heart especially goes out to the poor and needy. One of the most fascinating Scripture parts for all us Christians to ponder on occasionally is Matthew 25:31-46 where Jesus shows great solidarity with the poor and needy. Attending to their needs is *attending to Jesus*.

Wait, does this also have to do with the principle of sowing and reaping? Yes:

> *When you give to the poor, it is like lending to the LORD, and the LORD will pay you back.*
>
> *Proverbs 19:17 GNT*

> *He who gives to the poor will not lack,*
> *But he who hides his eyes will have many curses.*
>
> *Proverbs 28:27*

The Bible also says that an undeserved curse will not land (Proverbs 26:2). Do you know what this implies? That there are some *deserved* curses. Curses with a cause. Hiding your eyes for the poor will invoke not *few* but *many* curses. On the other hand, being generous leads you to many blessings (Proverbs 19:17, 22:9, Proverbs 28:27;). Makes it an easy choice to give, right? Remember, to not give or do good things to be seen, or you might lose your reward (Matthew 6:1-4).

Other principles of giving is sowing

The other principles are given by Apostle Paul in his letter to the Corinthian Church:

- *The seed should always be given out of love (1 Corinthians 13:3)*
- *The seed should not be a seed given out of extortion but voluntary (2 Corinthians 9:5)*
- *The seed should not be given grudgingly (2 Corinthians 9:7)*
- *The seed should be given purposefully (2 Corinthians 9:7)*
- *The seed should be given cheerfully (2 Corinthians 9:7)*

Don't just throw your seed in the ground and wait passively. Use all these principles, cultivate your ground, pray, seek God and do all the other necessary things that God requires from you. Use the key of sowing to be able to reap from the promises of God. Reap through your giving!

9. Ungodly Acquired Wealth is Harmful

A fortune made by a lying tongue
is a fleeting vapor and a deadly snare

Proverbs 21:6

Many times the Bible warns us not to envy the prosperity of the ungodly (Psalm 37:7). The principle of reaping and sowing does not only apply to giving but to every action (Galatians 6:7). God sees everything and is not to be mocked. Ungodly acquired wealth is harmful in many ways; in essence, it's a deadly snare.

The Bible says that calamity will befall those practicing illicit activities to gain wealth (Micah 2:1-5). In addition to that, God's Word says that riches that are gained ungodly are like a fleeting vapor (Proverbs 21:6). In other words, in a blink of an eye it's gone.

Wealth gained by dishonesty will be diminished,
But he who gathers by labor will increase.

Proverbs 13:11

One who increases his possessions by usury and extortion
Gathers it for him who will pity the poor.

Proverbs 28:8

A man with an evil eye hastens after riches

And does not consider that poverty will come upon him.

Proverbs 28:22

The righteous leave an inheritance for their children's children, the unrighteous leave if for the righteous (Proverbs 13:22; Job 27:16-17):

Though he heaps up silver like dust,
And piles up clothing like clay—
He may pile it up, but the just will wear it,
And the innocent will divide the silver.

Job 27:16-17

10. Hard Work is A Key To Wealth

He who has a slack hand becomes poor,
But the hand of the diligent makes rich.

Proverbs 10:4

The Amplified Bible translation says: *Lazy hands make for poverty, but diligent hands bring wealth (Proverbs 10:4).* Diligence means careful and persistent work or effort. Synonyms for diligent are active, attentive, careful, eager, industrious, tireless, unrelenting, careful and persistent.

So the Bible says that careful and persistent work is one of the keys to wealth. Are you performing your day to day activities in an attentive, careful, tireless and unrelenting manner? In other words, are you persisting in working hard and are you eager to keep on improving yourself in the smallest details? Discipline yourself to bring out your best performance.

Opportunity is missed by most people because it is dressed in overalls and looks like work. – Thomas Edison

Motivation to work hard

Hard work is easy when it comes through intrinsic motivation. Intrinsic motivation is the motivation that comes from within ourselves, where we do not need anyone to motivate us. I believe that when we do something we like we're easily motivated from within ourselves.

Need some motivation to do your work diligently? The Bible says to do all our work as working for the Lord (Colossians 3:23). That should be enough motivation to work diligently, right?

> *The sleep of a laboring man is sweet, whether he eats little or much.*
>
> *Ecclesiastes 5:12a*

Nothing better than knowing that you've worked hard, have done something valuable and lay your head down to rest. Sometimes we may not realize it but working gives us a certain fulfillment. Plus, are there any from rags to riches stories that exclude hard work? I doubt it.

Does heaven help those who help themselves?

Hard work is a key to wealth. So, all this time people that actually exclude God and say "heaven helps those who help themselves" were right? No, it's not merely your own effort that will bring wealth. Remember that God's eyes are even on the sparrow and that He cares for us in all ways (Matthew 10:29-31). He is involved in everything. That does not mean that we should cross our arms and just pray for food to come to our mouths. Even before the Fall, Adam needed to work in the garden of Eden (Genesis 2:15)!

On the other hand, the Bible also has many (negative) promises about laziness. One of the most striking images about the consequence of laziness comes from King Solomon: *a little sleep, a little slumber, a little folding of the hands to sleep. So shall your poverty come on you like a prowler (or thief), and your need like an armed man (Proverbs 6:10-11).* The Bible also says lazy hands make for poverty, but the hand of the diligent make rich (Proverbs 10:4). It is your decision: are you going to do everything you can to do your work diligently and thus claim God's promises concerning riches or will you continue to await your poverty as a thief and your lack as an armed man by remaining lazy and lying down with folded hands?

I believe hard work is the starting point for many blessings as it first develops the right attitude in us. Remember the Hebrew word for "to prosper"? *Tsalach. Tsalach* can also be translated as *to push forward.* I believe God's tailwind will push us forward to prosperity when we start moving diligently. Abraham, Joseph and the other prosperous ones were not lying down passively when God decided to prosper them!

I encourage you to use all the keys in God's Word concerning wealth in conjunction with each other to have a great effect. Hard work aids in acquiring wealth. Plus, the promises of God are upon hard work. Let this be our continual motivation: *And whatever you do, do it heartily, as to the Lord and not to men* (Colossians 3:23).

11. Smart Work is A Key To Wealth

Go to the ant, you sluggard!

Consider her ways and be wise,

Which, having no captain,

Overseer or ruler,

Provides her supplies in the summer,

And gathers her food in the harvest.

How long will you slumber, O sluggard

When will you rise from your sleep?

A little sleep, a little slumber,

A little folding of the hands to sleep—

So shall your poverty come on you like a prowler,

And your need like an armed man.

Proverbs 6:6-11

Hard work pays off. Actually, hard *and* smart work pays off even better. To reach this conclusion (Proverbs 6:6-11), Solomon studied a specific group: *ants.*

He considered their smart ways and became wiser through it.

1. Ants work efficiently together in a highly coordinated way

Ants perform their activities smartly and highly coordinated. Anyone studying ants notes that they live and work together as a team in extremely organized societies called colonies.

Ants function very efficiently as one body. Recent studies have discovered that their communication is also highly developed. They know their place and work together for a common goal, even without an overseer or ruler. Nobody needs to boss them around as each ant knows his position and function. Isn't that a beautiful thing we all can learn from?

2. Ants plan and are prepared for the future

There's no well-functioning company in the world that works without planning for the future. Then why do we oftentimes forget this as individuals? Managing wealth is a matter of anticipation of what may come. This is how the hardest blows can be absorbed and wealth is retained. Ants know that there are several seasons in a year. That's why they anticipate and prepare for future seasons. Well, that's smart work, that will bring *and* retain wealth.

3. Ants work hard even when there is plenty

In summer there is plenty of food for ants but this abundance does not create sluggish behavior in them. They know that in wintertime food could be scarce so they build up a buffer. They *invest* time (work extra hard) to be able to *save* up (which is smart work). Saving and investing, a wise and wealthy person knows all about it.

Hard work is good but do you also work efficiently, coordinated and do you have a clear plan and goal in mind? Are you prepared for what may come? Besides what we can learn from ants there are several other tips for smart work that focus on time management, productivity, agility etc. but the main point here is that smart work (+ hard work) is a key to wealth. *The plans (having a plan is smart work) of the diligent (hard and attentive working) lead to plenty (Proverbs 21:5a).* Work hard and smart and it will surely lead to plenty!

12. God-given Talents and Gifts Make Room for Wealth

As each one has received a gift, minister it to one another, as good

stewards of the manifold grace of God.

1 Peter 4:10

The Bible says that each one of us has received a gift from God. We *all* have received a gift. The word used in Greek for "gift" is the word *charisma*. *Charisma* is defined as a gift of grace; a favor that one receives without any merit of his own.

Do you see a man skillful in his work?
He will stand before kings;
He will not stand before obscure men.

Proverbs 22:29

I believe we'll be extraordinary skilled when we keep polishing our God-given talent and gifts by using them and by not sitting on them. Investing time *extraordinarily* will lead to *extraordinary* results. That is when we will become *extraordinarily* skillful and people will be willing to pay us *extraordinarily* for our *extraordinary* skills.

Have you ever seen a rough diamond cube? It looks similar to an ordinary stone but after cutting and sharpening through an intensive process, the brilliance of a diamond becomes visible. Like a diamond, every gift, whether spiritual or natural, should be sharpened and polished.

Are you wondering what your God-given talent and gifts are? Remember, we *all* have received a gift (1 Peter 4:10). We are fearfully (in other words, marvelously, remarkably, awesomely, amazingly) and wonderfully made (Psalm 139:13-14). We are His workmanship (Ephesians 2:10). The following three simple questions can help you discover your (natural) gifts and talents:

- What do others compliment you on?

- What were your best skills/subjects during your education?

- What can you do easily (and you feel as it were as a duck in water executing it) that others find challenging?

It has become a cliché but look at our unique DNA. Of all the 7 billion people on the earth and all that have ever walked on the face of this planet before, no one has the same fingerprint as you have. No one carries your uniqueness. God is a Master Designer. The Master Designer has given you a unique gift. Even the simplest gift that others also have, you embody your own unique style of execution. Dig deep inside yourself to discover this gift.

Remember, that we as human beings differ from each other, each has one received from God according to his own ability (Matthew 25:14). Please note: when it was time to judge his servants, the master never said: why did you only have an increase of 2 whilst the other servant had an increase of 5? In other words: don't compare yourself with others. We will all be judged on the basis of what we have received (based on our own abilities, a fish is not judged on its tree climbing abilities). Howard Gardner's multiple intelligence theory may also help us to see that we all may excel in different areas. I advise you to study that theory (just Google it for a sec or look it up on YouTube).

Brothers and sisters, let's use our God-given talents and gifts and help others with it. In the end, people are willing to reward us financially for the unique skillfulness that we exhibit! Let's do it with all our might (Ecclesiastes 9:10), not only to gather wealth but also so we can hear at the end of our lives: *"Well done, good and faithful servant; you have been faithful over a few things, I will make you ruler over many things. Enter into the joy of your lord (Matthew 25:23)."*

13. Wealth Will Not Provide You With Ultimate Security

Some trust in chariots, and some in horses; but we will remember the name of the Lord our God

Psalm 20:7

Horses and chariots were a sign of military power. The more you had, the stronger your army was. In addition to that, chariots and horses were also a sign of wealth. Only the wealthy and powerful military forces had numerous chariots and horses. King David definitely acquired a lot but he knew one thing: *wealth will never provide anyone with ultimate security*. As a young shepherd boy, he relied on God for his victory against Goliath. Even later on as a king, when his wealth had increased, he relied on God and knew *when riches increase, do not set your heart on them* (Psalm 62:10).

Jesus warned the people for the lies that wealth spreads (Matthew 13:22). One of the deceitful things that wealth spreads is that once you're wealthy, you're secure. In other words: who needs God when you have wealth?

Remember the story of the rich fool (Luke 12:16-21)?

> *Then He spoke a parable to them, saying: "The ground of a certain rich man yielded plentifully. And he thought within himself, saying, 'What shall I do, since I have no room to store my crops?' So he said, 'I will do this: I will pull down my barns and build greater, and there I will store all my crops and my goods. And I will say to my soul, "Soul, you have many goods laid up for many years; take your ease; eat, drink, and be merry.*
>
> *Luke 12:16-19*

Why was the rich man foolish? He thought that his goods would provide him with *ultimate* security for his present and future situation. He ignored God. *But God said to him, 'Fool! This night your soul will be required of you; then whose will those things be which you have provided?' "So is he who lays up treasure for himself, and is not rich toward God (Luke 12:20-21)"*.

Indeed those that trust in their riches will fall (Proverbs 11:28). When you are sick, your money might give you access to good healthcare but can it buy you healing? Can your riches purchase love (Songs of Solomon 8:7)? Can money buy you happiness? Ultimately, can you buy your way to heaven?

Do not be misled to hope in the uncertainty of riches (1 Timothy 6:17) but remember and trust in the only One that provides us with ultimate security.

14. Wealth Through Obeying and Seeking God

*Uzziah was sixteen years old when he became king, and he reigned fifty-two years in Jerusalem. His mother's name was Jecholiah of Jerusalem. And he did what was right in the sight of the Lord, according to all that his father Amaziah had done. He sought God in the days of Zechariah, who had understanding in the visions of God; **and as long as he sought the Lord, God made him prosper.***

2 Chronicles 26:3-5

As long as Uzziah sought the Lord, God made him prosper. I love this verse. It makes the link between seeking the Lord and prosperity extremely clear. But what kind of prosperity is the Bible talking about? 2 Chronicles 26:6-15 gives us an answer. Uzziah was successful in warfare against the Philistines and the Arabians.

Being successful in warfare always had a material side to it, as much spoil of wars was always taken. In addition, the Ammonites, traditionally enemies of Israel, brought tribute to him. Bringing tribute in this sense most probably meant a payment to King Uzziah as a mark of submission, in order to maintain peace and/or protection. So God's prosperity even made Uzziah's enemies to bring tribute to him. *When a man's ways please the LORD, he maketh even his enemies to be at peace with him (Proverbs 16:7).*

Uzziah became exceedingly strong and his fame grew. He built towers, dug wells (and succeeded in all of this as the Lord made him to prosper), had much livestock plus farmers and vinedressers. Seems like great prosperity right?

It's clear that Uzziah was not obliged to eat dry bread everyday. His prosperity list goes on. The Bible says *moreover,* he led a great army and was successful in making machines of war. Verse 15 (2 Chronicles 26) ends this part of Scripture by saying that Uzziah's name spread far abroad; *for he was marvelously helped (by God) until he was strong.*

So God made Uzziah prosper *as long as he sought Him.* Look at what an exceeding list of blessings this seeking of God brought forth. In contrast to that, everything immediately went downhill when pride entered Uzziah's heart and he stopped seeking and obeying the Lord.

> *Now it shall come to pass,* **if you diligently obey the voice** *of the Lord your God, to observe carefully all His commandments which I command you today, that the Lord your God will set you high above all nations of the earth. And all these blessings shall come upon you and overtake you, because you obey the voice of the Lord your God (Deuteronomy 28:1-2)*

You cannot separate seeking God from obeying Him. I believe that as long as Uzziah sought *to obey* the Lord, the Lord prospered him. You cannot obey Him without knowing what He wants, right? So you need to seek Him. God promised to bless the people of Israel if they would diligently obey Him. If they would obey God, the blessings would not only come upon them but also *overtake* them. I love that: the Lord's blessings can *overtake* you. The list of blessings in Deuteronomy 28 is wonderful. The key to all of that? *Obedience.*

> *But seek first the kingdom of God and His righteousness, and all these things shall be added to you.*
>
> *Matthew 6:33*

Matthew 6:33 is a very well-known verse of the Bible. It says that when we make seeking (the kingdom of) God and His righteousness our top priority, things shall be added to us. This verse confirms that He will prosper us when we seek Him.

We should not seek God for the sole reason that He gives us things. We should always seek the Giver and not the gift. That being said, he who comes to God must believe that He is, and that He is a rewarder of those who diligently seek Him (Hebrews 11:6)! Seek Him and believe that you will be rewarded! His rewards are inevitable.

15. Wealth Should Not Dominate Your Heart

Above all else, guard your heart,
for everything you do flows from it

Proverbs 4:23

A wise man should have money in his head, but not in his heart.
-Jonathan Swift

The Bible encourages us to keep track of our wealth to manage it properly (Proverbs 27:23-24). So in that sense, money should be in our head (of course in a healthy manner). Money in our heart is a different matter. We're encouraged to guard our hearts with all diligence, for out of it spring the issues of life (Proverbs 4:23).

Bible commentators have also translated Proverbs 4:23 as *keep thy heart with all keeping*. With all diligence, so, above all things that have to be guarded, keep or guard thy heart. Guard all the things which are advantageous for you, for example, your health, body, riches, property, but before and above everything else, keep a guard on your heart. Jesus said that out of the heart evil thoughts and all sorts of evil things proceed (Matthew 15:19). There lies a danger in these evil things entering your heart when not guarded properly. Do you know which evil relating to wealth can enter? *Greed.* Greed can easily enter when wealth dominates our hearts.

The (extreme) love of money (in other words, greed) is one of the things that should not be allowed to enter the gates of our hearts. Greed is to be pictured as a ferocious beast. It leaves little room for other things to love in your heart and devours principles and morals like they've never existed.

All the issues of life depend on the condition of our hearts. If our hearts are pure, our lives and motives will be pure; if our hearts are corrupt, our lives and motives will be corrupt. If money dominates our heart all our actions will be centered around making money. Our priority will then not be the interest of God's Kingdom, nor the well-being of our fellow brothers or sisters, nor the interest of our environment.

All principles and morals are thrown overboard as soon as wealth dominates our hearts. Fellow brothers and sisters, my prayer is that you will guard your heart with all diligence and that you may keep your conduct free from greed (Hebrews 13:5).

16. Wealth Should Not Puff Up

As for the rich in this present world, instruct them not to be conceited and arrogant, nor to set their hope on the uncertainty of riches, but on God, who richly and ceaselessly provides us with everything for our enjoyment.

1 Timothy 6:17 AMP

The Apostle Paul commands Timothy to instruct the rich to not be conceited and arrogant (1 Timothy 6). Being conceited is being excessively proud of oneself. Someone who's arrogant has or reveals an exaggerated sense of one's own importance or abilities. Conceit and arrogance have to do with one thing: *ego.* Ourselves.

When our ego steps in the way, we are not able to see others (and their needs). Our inflated egos might even prevent us from seeing and hearing God clearly. God resists the proud but gives grace to the humble (1 Peter 5:5). We are to do nothing through selfish ambition or conceit, but in lowliness of mind let each esteem others better than himself (Philippians 2:3-4).

Why is the warning for conceit and arrogance particularly directed towards the rich? If one isn't paying attention, riches can become an enormous boost for our ego. There awaits a danger, especially when rich, to become proud and think that our intelligence or our talent, gave us the right to become rich. Wealth has the ability to puff up someone's ego and make one arrogant. The wrong thinking is: I'm wealthy just because I deserve it, others that are not, just don't deserve it.

Once people start increasing their riches and are able to buy expensive houses, cars and clothes, there lies a danger in believing to be worth more than others. A feeling of superiority can easily creep into us. After that, the next step to downfall is then to neglect God and start trusting in riches. Remember, pride comes before a fall (1 Corinthians 10:12).

Need an antidote against selfish, conceited and arrogant thinking? It's quite simple: acknowledge God as the one that gave you (the power to make) wealth. *For who makes you differ from another? And what do you have that you did not receive? Now if you did indeed receive it, why do you boast as if you had not received it (1 Corinthians 4:7).* When we sincerely acknowledge Him as the Giver and keep our focus on Him, our hearts will ultimately remain humble.

17. Wealth is To Be Distributed

*But whoever has this world's goods, and sees his brother in need,
and shuts up his heart from him, how does the love of God abide in
him?*

1 John 3:17 AMP

Sharing is caring. Wealth is God's blessing and should be enjoyed by us. But not only by ourselves.

The Early Church had all things in common, sold their possessions and distributed to others (Acts 2:44-45; 4:34). I'm not insisting that God says that we should follow this example and sell all of our possessions but we should never forget to share. Remember that Ananias and his wife Sapphira were not punished because they didn't want to share all their proceeds from their sale, but because they lied to the Holy Ghost about it.

Do you know that your motives to distribute wealth can even determine whether you will receive wealth?

> *You ask [God for something] and do not receive it, because you ask*
> *with wrong motives [out of selfishness or with an unrighteous*
> *agenda], so that [when you get what you want] you may spend it on*
> *your [hedonistic] desires*

> *James 4:3 AMP*

Hedonistic desires are desires where you place yourself and your own pleasures first. We, as Christians, should care for others around us. Apostle John asks a powerful question: how can the love of God abide in us if we do not show it in deeds (1 John 3:17)? Sharing is even something that benefits yourself, remember the 8th truth we have covered: *giving (to share) is also a form of sowing.*

With whom should you share? This question reminds me of the question "who is my neighbor" after Jesus said "love thy neighbor as thyself" in Luke 10. The answer is similar: every fellow human being. We should be willing to share with practically every fellow human being (not only with our brothers, sisters and loved ones). However, God's heart especially goes out to the poor and needy (for example Proverbs 19:17) and widows and orphans (Deuteronomy 14:28-29). Are we as Christians making sure to actively support these groups with our finances?

> *Let him who stole steal no longer, but rather let him labor, working*
> *with his hands what is good, that he may have something to give him*
> *who has need.*

> *Ephesians 4:28*

Why do we actually work? For money, enjoyment, fulfillment? Paul gives another reason, so that we may have something to give to those who are in need! In many modern societies, welfare systems are set up, so we actually share with the needy via taxes, but as these systems are not perfect, I believe we can still do more to share from our abundance! Never forget to do good and to share, for with such sacrifices God is well pleased (Hebrews 13:16)!

18. Wealth Is Not Merely Attached To Your Level of Faith or Righteousness

For you yourselves know how you ought to follow our example, because we did not act in an undisciplined or inappropriate manner when we were with you [we were never idle or lazy, nor did we avoid our duties], nor did we eat anyone's bread without paying for it, but with labor and hardship we worked night and day [to pay our own way] so that we would not be a financial burden on any of you [for our support];

2 Thessalonians 3:7-8 AMP

The Apostle Paul was a tentmaker (Acts 18:1-3). He said to the church in Thessalonica that he worked with labor and hardship night and day to pay his own way. Remember, this is the man that received a very special assignment of God and wrote about 30% of the New Testament. This shows us the mindset that Paul had. He acknowledged that the Lord's servants are entitled to financial rewards but sometimes refused to receive them (2 Corinthians 12:14).

What am I trying to say with this? Somehow, one of the untruths concerning wealth that is spread is that Christians who aren't wealthy simply do not have enough faith (for example to sow significantly) or are just not righteous enough. The life of Paul completely falsifies this train of thought. I am sure that Paul could have been very wealthy even because of all the donations people must have wanted to give him due to all the extraordinary miracles they saw performed through his hands (Acts 19:11). At more than one instance, people considered him to be the embodiment of one of the (false) gods and even sacrifices were brought to him (Acts 14:8-18; Acts 28:6). But he didn't care too much for these rewards as he learned to be content (Philippians 4:11-12).

What the Bible actually says:

- Being wealthy or not has to do with our attitude. For example, like Paul, some of us simply don't want to be wealthy (see Proverbs 30).

- Faith could have to do with wealth as it the basis for claiming promises. This doesn't mean that only through faith wealth is claimed. There are also other steps to follow. The same applies to righteousness or for the principle of giving.

- The thought "the more righteous you are, the more wealth you must have" is false. This claim seems to have no biblical basis. Was Solomon the wealthiest man because he had the greatest faith or was the most righteous man? There is no biblical evidence that supports that thinking.

Is there a connection between wealth, faith and righteousness? Yes, I do believe there is. In the house of the righteous, there is much treasure

(Proverbs 15:6). The righteous shall live by faith (Romans 1:17). The righteousness of God is by faith (Romans 3:22). But does that inherently mean that the more faith one has and the more righteous a man is, the more his wealth must be? No. There are other keys to follow to accumulate wealth. The truth shall set us free (John 8:32).

Claiming in faith

Wealth is not *merely* attached to our faith, however as I mentioned before, faith is our basis for claiming promises (thus also concerning wealth) and is the currency in God's Kingdom. If we want something from God we need faith, we can't please Him without faith (Hebrews 11:6). Can a Christian pray for riches? Of course, we can, in a healthy manner of course. Isn't wealth a good gift when given to a mature and pure hearted person?

Which of you, if your son asks for bread, will give him a stone? Or if he asks for a fish, will give him a snake? If you, then, though you are evil, know how to give good gifts to your children, how much more will your Father in heaven give good gifts to those who ask him!

Matthew 7:9-11

A major obstacle in receiving answer to all of our prayers (including our prayers concerning our finances) is found in James 4:2: *you do not have because you do not ask.*

So, do we actually sincerely ask God in faith for an increase of our finances? James 4:3 warns us that we will not even receive something when our motives are wrong, however asking for wealth could be done with the right motives! Do we actually pray and claim the promises in

God's Word concerning wealth when we give our seed, offerings, give to the needy, when we lend, when we sacrifice, when we steward His finances correctly according to His Word? I believe us to be *highly* effective in prayer when we go back to God with His own words, His promises! Do you know that Elijah (a man subject to passions like us; James 5:17) actually stopped it from raining for 3,5 years based on a promise in Deuteronomy (read chapter 11)? We need to be aware of the spiritual reality we live in. The effective, fervent prayer of the righteous avails much (James 5:16)! No need to be sad if you have not claimed the promises in faith in the past yet, as God never forgets and we also have *retroactive* effect on our side!

Let's end in prayer: *Father God, we thank You for Your wonderful Word we can rely on. We thank You for the wonderful promises in the area of finances. Lord, we know that You cannot lie. Your Word says that we may not have because we do not ask. That's why we ask and stand in faith right now. We claim all Your promises concerning wealth. Lord, we claim all the blessings related to giving to You. We also claim everything we have sown in the past, with retroactive effect. If we have found favor in Your sight, Lord, do not pass us by in the area of finances. Open Your floodgates in the area of wealth over us and may we never forget the advancement of Your Kingdom. In Jesus' name we pray, amen.*

19. Wealth and Attitude Are Connected

Remove falsehood and lies far from me; Give me neither poverty nor riches — Feed me with the food allotted to me; Lest I be full and deny You, And say, "Who is the Lord?" Or lest I be poor and steal, And profane the name of my God.

Proverbs 30:8-9

The above words are taken from Proverbs 30:8-9 and are spoken by a man named Agur, the son of Jakeh. Agur did not want wealth as he was afraid to forget God once he had it. I believe that, assuming he prayed in faith, he received an answer to his prayer. Due to his heart condition concerning money, and his prayer that came forth out it, he was not wealthy. How many of us of that do desire to be wealthy, actually have an attitude or mindset that is in line with our desire?

Once I heard a man of God jokingly say that Agur himself said that he was more stupid than any other man (Proverbs 30:2-3) and that based on Agur's own account we shouldn't follow him. But there are others in the Bible too who did not receive or attain wealth because of their attitude or mindset. The Apostle Paul is one of those examples.

Apostle Paul's example

Paul indicated several times that he learned to live with or without prosperity. Please note that Paul was never hindered in fulfilling his mission for God by a lack of resources. It seems that he didn't care much for his finances; and in some cases, he even disregarded rewards for the purpose of the Kingdom of God.

With the help of Paul's example, I also shortly want to point out something that does not directly have to do with our attitude to be able to receive (more) wealth but has more to do with what the right biblical attitude is towards requesting for, accepting and handling money. By studying Apostle Paul's mindset we can also see that the Kingdom of God really was his first priority (and becoming rich was not) as he knew that asking for money could be a stumbling block for some (as they would then probably question his motives for preaching the gospel) or that his credibility or his ability to do what he wanted could be affected in some circles (like the Corinthian Church; 1 Corinthians 9) if he would request or accept their money. In addition to that, sometimes by refusing money, Paul wanted to be an example of someone with a good work ethic (2 Thessalonians 3:6-12).

Especially ministers in the Kingdom of God need to be wise and aware of their attitude towards the acceptance and handling of (a lot of) money, and certain lifestyles that can accompany wealth as they have the capacity to change people's view concerning someone. Be aware of the fact that when you handle money that primarily comes from donations (like offerings and tithes in the church), donators and other stakeholders will judge you on how you handle money. That's a fact. This is especially true for all handling of money by those involved in public institutions or non-profit organizations. Wouldn't you be surprised if someone leading the small non-profit organization that you donate to, obviously lives very extravagantly? It does not have to mean that the person uses the donated money in a wrong way but you can easily see how motives will be questioned and how one can lose credibility. Sometimes, we ought to take Paul's lifestyle choices and mindset as an example so we won't form an obstacle block for people to enter the Kingdom of God. Personally, I believe that how ministers have been involved in requesting for and handling money has done a lot of damage to the Kingdom of God and we need to keep on considering our ways. Remember, how wealthy one is does not only have to do with spiritual power, level of faith or righteousness and this equally applies to ministers of God.

That being said and moving on, in essence, I believe how wealthy one becomes has a lot to do with attitude and mindset. It is an individual's choice. Is it wrong to reject wealth? Not per se, sometimes it's a good thing, like Paul's example shows us. However, I do believe that we are held accountable when we let go of God-given opportunities to increase our wealth, especially when we claim to be restricted by our financial situation in fulfilling our missions for the Kingdom. Also, I believe it is good when we're able to say that we have enough but shouldn't we surpass looking only at our own needs? Why should we give up on opportunities to make more if one of the benefits of having more than enough is that we then can easily invest in the Kingdom and share with others?

Apostle James also makes clear that there is a negative attitude concerning wealth which will prevent us from receiving it. A negative attitude concerning wealth is when we ask for it with the wrong motives and want to receive it for the wrong purposes:

> *You ask [God for something] and do not receive it, because you ask with wrong motives [out of selfishness or with an unrighteous agenda], so that [when you get what you want] you may spend it on your [hedonistic] desires.*

> *James 4:3 AMP*

I also believe that by having the wrong mindset we tend to overlook all the opportunities God presents to us to become wealthy. Being open-minded towards wealth is one of the first steps to receive it. Becoming wealthy is seldom something that *just* happens to someone. One needs to spot opportunities, which is very hard with a closed mind, and work towards them with the grace of God. Do you know which emotion prevented the lazy and wicked servant from spotting opportunities? *Fear*. I deem fear to be one of the strongest emotions that closes our mind and prevents us from seeing and hearing clearly. I'll go into fear deeper in the next chapter.

Poverty mindset

As a man thinks so is he (Proverbs 23:7). This tells us a lot about the importance of our mindset.

"Watch your thoughts, they become your words; watch your words,

they become your actions; watch your actions, they become your habits; watch your habits, they become your character; watch your character, it becomes your destiny." – Lao Tzu

I believe there to be something like a "poverty mindset" which is a way of thinking that makes it extremely difficult to become wealthy. People with a poverty mindset may have got it since childhood as they have seen their parents struggle with money and have the belief that they will never become rich and think in obstacles instead of possibilities. Thinking "poor" (being close-minded) may block what God has prepared for us.

As Christians we need to be aware that this thinking may also be influenced by spiritual forces. For we do not wrestle against flesh and blood (Ephesians 6:12). Through prayer and God's Word we can get rid of every wrong thinking.

If our minds are set on the Kingdom and we are not only focused on ourselves and hedonistic purposes, I am convinced that the windows of heaven will be open and many (financial) blessings will be bestowed upon us. When we focus our minds on God's Kingdom, we will also have more financiers who will direct (more of) their finances to God's Work.

Think about it: how much more could your church be doing to minister in your neighborhood, in your community, in your city, in your nation, and around the world if more funds were available? Suppose your church's income was multiplied overnight by five or even by two. Could your church then have a greater impact in reaching more souls (for example television networks or radio stations can be reached or even launched), ministering to more saints (for example by spreading more teaching material), helping more poor people, or financing more missionaries? I think the answer is clear.

As our attitude or mindset can be a key determinant in whether we will even receive wealth, we should start by setting it right. Brothers and sisters, if we desire to be wealthy for Kingdom purposes, keep on working on and praying for the right attitude and mindset.

20. Fear is a Wealth Blocker

Then the man who had received one bag of gold came. 'Master,' he said, 'I knew that you are a hard man, harvesting where you have not sown and gathering where you have not scattered seed. **So I was afraid** *and went out and hid your gold in the ground. See, here is what belongs to you.*

Matthew 25:24-25

The parable of the talents is well-known. A certain master gives his servants talents of money and leaves the city for a while. He expects his servants to do business until he returns and to multiply what they have received. Upon the master's return, two of the three servants doubled what they had received, but one of the servants was an exception as he decided to hide his talent of money in the ground. What was this particular servant's reason for hiding his talent? The reason is simple: *fear*. Matthew 25:25 gives us this answer.

Fear prevented the one servant from thinking straight and seeing business opportunities. Fear even prevented the servant from putting the money with the bankers so he could receive interest, which is one of the simplest forms, even nowadays, to receive an increase of money. Fear paralyzes. *Fear is a wealth blocker.*

Everything you want is on the other side of fear. – Jack Canfield

> *Be strong and of good courage; do not be afraid, nor be dismayed, fore the LORD your God is with you wherever you go*
>
> *Joshua 1:9*

Joshua was standing in front of the Jordan with the people of Israel when God spoke these words to him. Do you know what God actually said to Joshua? The promised land that you and the people want to take in is on the other side of the Jordan *but also* on the other side of fear. *Conquer that fear and you will get what you want. I, the Lord, will be with you.*

Do you know that the lazy and wicked servant even had a special kind of fear? Fear of other people. To be specific, fear of what others might think or say. Fear (of other's opinions) has the ability to prevent us from reaching our full potential. Fear has the ability to take ground in your thought life and dictate you to hide your talents in the ground. That is, of course when you give fear the chance to do so.

What is fear? it has been said that fear is negative faith. The definition of faith is found in the Bible in Hebrews 11. Based on this definition of faith in Hebrews 11:1 we can also come to the definition of *negative* faith:

> *Now fear is based on the (mostly) false assurance that your mind forms of things you are afraid of, and the false evidence of things not seen [the false conviction of their reality—fear wants to take as fact what is*

not even experienced by the physical senses].

This definition clarifies how fear can block wealth. Fear has the ability to form false convictions in the realm of your mind which may seem very real. You might think there are certain barriers on your way to wealth while these are not even real and only exist in our minds!

Think about it for a second. What idea have you had for years but haven't brought to life because of a fear to fail? What idea have you tried to suppress in your mind because you are afraid of what others might think or say? What idea do you have to increase wealth which a false conviction in your mind is preventing from coming into existence? Of course, risk is attached to certain ideas we have and I certainly advise to assess these risks properly before taking action. However, many times fear even disturbs our risk assessment capabilities and makes mountains seem a lot bigger in our minds.

We suffer more in imagination than in reality. – Seneca

So, how do we overcome fear?

First of all, remember that fear is not of God (2 Timothy 1:7). Many times fear is just imagination and something that only lives in our minds. And everything that is not of God and thus comes from the enemy, we need to reject.

With our weapons of warfare (prayer, praise and worship, the Word of God, proclamations and more) we ought to cast down imaginations and bring into captivity every thought to the obedience of Christ (2 Corinthians 10:4-5). Every thought of fear (imagination) we ought to cast down. Rest in the assurance of God's promises about fear in His

Word and let it sink into your heart until these promises become a real conviction in your heart.

All of us received gifts and talents. Like the servants in the parable of the talents, we have received much. Many times however, we act like the lazy and wicked servant by walking around with these gifts and talents without using them because of our fear of failure. Fearing what others might think of us when we fall. Fear to step out and take risks. Think about it like this: if we are afraid to use our gifts and talents then how can we end up standing before kings (Proverbs 22:29)? The same applies to money, if we are even frightened to invest when (small) risk is attached to it, then how will we multiply our money?

> *He who watches the wind [waiting for all conditions to be perfect] will not sow [seed], and he who looks at the clouds will not reap [a harvest].*

> *Ecclesiastes 11:4 AMP*

> *For God did not give us a spirit of timidity or cowardice or fear, but [He has given us a spirit] of power and of love and of sound judgment and personal discipline [abilities that result in a calm, well-balanced mind and self-control].*

> *2 Timothy 1:7*

We did not receive a spirit of fear. Fear is not of God. I love how the Amplified Bible Translation puts it: we have received the abilities that result in a calm, well-balanced mind and self-control. What else do we need? Cast out that wealth blocker named fear and go for it!

21. Wealth Comes Through Obedience and Positioning

*And He has made from one blood every nation of men to dwell on all the face of the earth, and **has determined their preappointed times and the boundaries of their dwellings.***

Acts 17:26

The Bible clearly says that God positions us in time and location (Acts 17:26). Do you know how to be at the right place and the right time? It's simple, just listen to God's voice. Europe has played a major role in the spreading of the Gospel. Do you actually know how the first apostle came to Europe? It was the result of a direct call from God, through a vision, that Paul obeyed (Acts 16:6-10). It resulted in a great outpouring of the Lord's saving grace in the continent of Europe. Obeying God's positioning is highly important in receiving His favor.

I truly believe that obeying God's voice in positioning us is also important for our financial well-being. Let's look at two examples:

Abraham and his son Isaac. Abraham's example is simple. The Lord told him that he would become a great nation, would bless him, make his name great and make him to be a blessing. *But,* the prophecy was conditional. First, he needed to get out of his country and get away from his family to a land that God would show him. Abraham needed to obey God's positioning *and then* the blessings would come upon him (Genesis 12:1-2). Sometimes, this can mean that we may have to leave our (locational and cultural) comfort zone.

Abraham left all behind. His known environment, his father's house for a land that was unknown to him. Ur could have been a wonderful place that he enjoyed. He might have enjoyed the comfort of his father's house(hold) and the presence of his loved ones around him very much. However, he left this comfort zone when God told him to do that. This is a key to prosperity. When we are sent out by God, do we check our comfort situation first or do we just obey by faith, knowing that He will bring us into an even greater position?

Then the example of Isaac. Isaac lived in Canaan and never left. This is what the Bible records about Isaac's prosperity;

> *Then Isaac sowed **in that land**, and reaped in the same year a hundredfold; and the Lord blessed him. The man began to prosper, and continued prospering until he became very prosperous; for he had possessions of flocks and possessions of herds and a great number of servants. So the Philistines envied him.*
>
> *Genesis 26:12-14*

Do you know what was recorded before this great account of Isaac's prosperity? When there was a famine in the land, the Bible records that Isaac decided to leave Canaan and go down to Egypt with his entire household. But look at what happened:

> Then the LORD appeared to him and said: "Do not go down to Egypt; live in the land of which I shall tell you. **Dwell in this land, and I will be with you and bless you**; for to you and your descendants I give all these lands, and I will perform the oath which I swore to Abraham your father.

> *Genesis 26:2-3*

Isaac obeyed to dwell at that location and prospered greatly when he sowed there.

Are the blessings of the Most High limited to location? Of course not. However, it can be God's specific will for your life to remain at or move to a certain location and this can be decisive in your prosperity.

God's voice in leading you to a certain location for opportunities can even be very specific. Remember how Jesus directed Simon Peter when he was fishing? Peter and his crew toiled the entire night but did not catch anything. However, when Jesus positioned them correctly and they obeyed, they caught so many fish that the nets broke! Jesus' directions of positioning even led Peter to money in the mouth of a fish (Matthew 17:26-27)!

Sometimes God's voice comes through His servants. The Bible records a story in 2 Kings 4 where a woman, whose husband had died, was about to give up her sons to slavery in order to pay off debt. She positioned herself correctly by going to the prophet Elisha for help and the prophet gave this woman a prophetic instruction. When the woman obeyed, she tapped into God's supernatural provision and a miracle of multiplication happened. She was able to not only pay off her debt, but even tapped into abundance as she even received extra to get by with!

What was the widow's first key? Positioning. She positioned herself in the close proximity of the prophet and through him she could obey God's voice. Her second key was obedience. The woman exactly did what the man of God instructed her to do.

> *Believe in the Lord your God, and you shall be established; believe His prophets, and you shall prosper.*

> *2 Chronicles 20:20b*

Be encouraged that, like the woman in 2 Kings 4 that was pushed forward, God's words are able to bring you from a position of lack into His favor. Keep your ears and eyes open to what God is revealing to you. Be diligent to completely obey His instructions and see how cycles of lack are instantly broken, and tap into His supernatural provision for your life!

In the widow's case, it was all about positioning herself in the vicinity of a certain person to become prosperous. However, it could also work the other way around: positioning yourself *out* of the vicinity of a certain person. Evil company corrupts good habits (1 Corinthians 15:33), this is also applicable in the area of finances. As iron sharpens iron, so one man sharpens another (Proverbs 27:17), so choose those "sharp" individuals around you that will push you to do better in the area of finances.

In the Bible we can find a clear example of how someone's presence can block another man's blessing. We have covered how Abraham was directed to leave his family behind. I believe he needed to leave the wrong practices, like idolatry (Joshua 24:2), in his father's house that blocked the Lord's entrance. Abraham was instructed to leave his family behind *but* he still decides to take his nephew Lot with him. Was this in line with God's directions? I do know that the Bible clearly says the following:

> The LORD *said to Abram,* **after** *Lot had left him,* "**Now lift up your eyes and look** *from the place where you are standing, northward and southward and eastward and westward;*

> Genesis 13:14

Lift up your eyes and look. In the book of Genesis, God spoke to Abraham two times before this occasion noted in Genesis 13:14, however this is the first time God specifically says to Abraham *to lift up his eyes and look.* When did God say that to Abraham? *After* Lot had left him. You know what the name Lot means? *Veil* or *covering.* It makes me believe that Lot's departure meant an uncovering of the veil or covering on Abraham's eyes. Yes, Abraham was already blessed during the time Lot was with him but I believe that after the departure of Lot, God took the blessings upon Abraham to another dimension. In other words, you may need to move away from some people in your vicinity as they may cover (the fullness of) your blessing!

Remember that His sheep obey His voice (John 10:27). We ought to listen to His voice for divine positioning in order to prosper. You might read this and think that's all nice, but how can I hear God's voice myself? That's a whole other teaching and many has been said and written about this but just some basic tips. How do you recognize somebody's voice? Because you know that person. Get to know Him, be in regular contact with Him through prayer and His Word and in this way build up your relationship with Him. I am sure that if you will diligently seek Him you will find Him and hear His voice (Jeremiah 29:13)!

22. Wealth Comes Through Obedience and the Right Timing

To everything there is a season, A time for every purpose under heaven.

Ecclesiastes 3:1

The beginning of Ecclesiastes 3 is often cited: There is a time and season for everything. I like how the Good News Translation puts it: *Everything that happens in this world happens at the time God chooses.*

We ought to realize that everything happens according to God's timing. *Everything.* Some might wonder, what is the right timing? It's simple: *God's timing.* God's timing is perfect (Ecclesiastes 3:11). We learn what God's timing is, in the same way that we learn to recognize the Shepherd's voice: by having a relationship with Him (John 10:27).

Then David said to Abiathar the priest, Ahimelech's son, "Please bring the ephod here to me." And Abiathar brought the ephod to David. So David inquired of the Lord, saying, "Shall I pursue this troop? Shall I overtake them?" And He answered him, "Pursue, for you shall surely overtake them and without fail recover all."

1 Samuel 30:7-8

As I truly believe that obeying God's voice in positioning us *location-wise* impacts our financial well-being, I also believe God's voice in positioning us *time-wise* can impact our finances. God's positioning in location and time often go hand in hand. Let's look at the examples of Abraham and Isaac again. Would the Lord's blessing remain with them if they would have postponed their obedience? *"Well, listen God, I will obey You but just not now. This just doesn't come at a good time now. I first have to settle a few things before I can decide on moving or staying. Please bear with me God."*

Could you imagine that? The conditions for His blessing sure have to do with timing. For all we know, it could be that if Peter waited 15 minutes longer with casting out the nets, all the fish were long gone already!

There is a time to plant and a time to pluck what is planted (Ecclesiastes 3:2). In other words, there is a proper time for reaping and sowing. A farmer that plants an apple tree, normally does not expect it to be fully grown the next day. The farmer may need to cultivate the seed for several seasons before something comes out of it. There might be a season of "purging or pruning" (John 15:2) but in the end, when the right things are sown and it is cultivated right, fruit needs to start coming forth eventually.

Our God works with seasons. It seems simple, in harvest season you should reap, right? But when we're talking about wealth, how do we discern when it's harvesting or reaping season? In that case, it's not just as simple as waiting for one of the four seasons in a year to arrive. Like the sons of Issachar (1 Chronicles 12:32) we need to be able to recognize these seasons spiritually so we will not want to reap when it is actually sowing season. I sincerely believe that if we are at God's appointed place at God's appointed time we will receive His tailwind for prosperity! Let us pray continually that we will correctly discern His appointed time, so we will throw out our nets at the perfect time.

23. Stewarding Wealth is a Major Key

Both riches and honor come from You, And You reign over all.
In Your hand is power and might; In Your hand it is to make great
And to give strength to all.

1 Chronicles 29:12

At the end of his life, King David intended to build a highly impressive temple for God. After gathering gifts from the people he uttered beautiful words of prayer: both riches and honor come from you, and you reign over all. He also exclaimed: *O LORD our God, all this abundance that we have prepared to build You a house for Your holy name is from Your hand, and is all Your own (1 Chronicles 29:16).* These words of prayer tell us that David knew one great principle: the principle of *stewardship.*

A steward is someone that is appointed to manage or look after another's property. The principle of stewardship simply means that we realize that we're just managing or looking after *God's* wealth.

Understanding the principle of stewardship makes it a lot easier to give to God. Also in a more cheerful way. David understood that we never give to God, we always *give back* to God. The earth is the Lord's and the fulness thereof (Psalm 24:1). Everything we have comes from Him.

The parable of the talents (Matthew 25:14-30) clearly depicts how stewarding wealth is an important key in understanding wealth management and increasing wealth. The Bible says that a man went out of town and *entrusted* his servants with five, two and one talent(s). I like the word *entrusted*. When you entrust someone with something it has another dimension to it than just giving someone something or even lending. When you entrust someone with something, you give something (temporarily) in good trust to someone, expecting them to not to misuse it. It is important to note that God *entrusts* us with things and does not just *give* things to us. When something is *entrusted* to you, like God *entrusts* us with gifts, talents and finances, good stewardship is automatically expected! Moving on with the parable, when the man returned, he saw that only one servant did not double what he had. In fact, that one servant did absolutely nothing with his talent. But, I would like to zoom in on what the master did next. The master came back and rewarded the one that had ten talents with the one talent that was hid in the ground! And so he punished the "slothful" servant. He used this rule:

> *"For to everyone who has [and values his blessings and gifts from God, and has used them wisely], more will be given, and [he will be richly supplied so that] he will have an abundance; but from the one who does not have [because he has ignored or disregarded his blessings and gifts from God], even what he does*

have will be taken away.

Matthew 25:29 AMP

The Amplified Bible translation emphasizes that good stewardship is the key to *more* (material) gifts and blessings. In addition to that, I believe good stewardship is also a major key for:

- *Combating stinginess towards God in our hearts (as we realize He gave it to us first)*

- *Giving cheerfully to God without grudge (2 Corinthians 9:7)*

- *Overall joy and contentment in life due to a more grateful heart*

- *Humility (1 Corinthians 4:7)*

Did you know that how we handle wealth is even decisive in whether we will be entrusted with spiritual riches? When I first realized that I was astonished but that's what Jesus says!

> *Therefore if you have not been faithful in the unrighteous mammon, who will commit to your trust the* **true** *riches?*

Luke 16:11

True riches are meant to mean spiritual riches. Luke 16:1-12 tells the story of an unjust steward. The steward had managed his business as to secure future comfort for himself so that he was even safe beyond the time he had his position as steward. Jesus praises him for this action. So, Jesus says to use our property as *to secure happiness and comfort beyond our time on earth* (Luke 16:9). Besides the rule that handling earthly wealth determines spiritual wealth, three other interesting points echo throughout the story of the unjust steward:

1. If we are not faithful with small amounts of money, can God trust us with a lot of money (Luke 16:10)?

2. If we are not faithful with another person's money, can God give us our own (Luke 16:12)?

3. If we are not faithful with other people's businesses or property, will God give us our own (Luke 16:12)?

So we see that the principle of stewardship is a major key in correct Christian wealth management and is important in the eyes of God. Be encouraged by the riches of His promises concerning good stewardship. Let us strive to meet His conditions so He can add more and more to us!

24. Wealth is The Lord's Blessing

*The blessing of the Lord makes one **rich**,*

And He adds no sorrow with it.

Proverbs 10:22

The blessing of the Lord **makes one rich**. In Hebrew, the word *ashar* is used for "to make rich". This word is used 17 times in the Old Testament and in all instances it has to do with material prosperity!

If wealth comes into the hands of those who are not financially ethical and crave to get rich with a compulsive, greedy longing for it, wealth can be a trap. It may cause them to fall into many foolish things that will plunge people into ruin and destruction (1 Timothy 6:9 AMP).

Many that despise wealth view big multinational corporations automatically as institutions full of money-hungry people that have attained wealth by not sparing the environment, anything or anyone.

Wealthy individuals are also often frowned upon with judgmental remarks like, "O, I bet they do not pay their taxes like us or they must be involved in illegal practices". Of course, there are companies and persons, who do attain wealth in the wrong way. However, having wealth does not automatically mean that you *must* have secured it in a financially unethical way with a heart full of greed and that on your pursuit of wealth you must have been ruthless, destroyed many lives and the environment with it. Given to mature and pure-hearted Christians, wealth is the Lord's blessing and He will add no sorrow to it (Proverbs 10:22)! So we ought to make sure not to despise the Lord's wonderful blessing.

Take the wonderful men of God as examples like Abraham, Isaac, Jacob, Solomon, Job, Daniel and the more that were blessed by riches but did not let it get into their hearts. Remember, money isn't the root of all kinds of evil but the *love of* money (1 Timothy 6:10).

25. Wealth Is A Blessing, Not An Idol

No one can serve two masters. Either you will hate the one and love the other, or you will be devoted to the one and despise the other. You cannot serve both God and money.

Matthew 6:24 NIV

The King James Translation says you cannot serve God and *Mammon*. Mammon is an idol. An idol of money, wealth and material possessions, in other words *materialism*. I believe Jesus personified riches as Mammon in the Sermon of the Mount as an idol intentionally. I believe there's a spirit behind it that is able to entice when we do not guard our hearts diligently (Proverbs 4:23). That's when a blessing can become an idol.

The Amplified Bible translates it as: *You cannot serve God and mammon [money, possessions, fame, status, or whatever is valued more than the Lord].* Fame and status are usually attached to great wealth. With wealth, fame and status come (possessions are essentially the same). But remember, wealth is a blessing (Proverbs 10:22), but it should not be worshipped.

Did you notice how the Amplified Bible makes "whatever is valued more than the Lord" an alternative translation of Mammon? Anything you give more precious attention than God can become an idol in your heart. Material possessions could easily be placed higher than God in our contemporary society. Do you know that greed is even called idolatry? Read Colossians 3:5. Greed is called idolatry because it can replace our devotion to God.

How do we prevent riches to take over in our hearts? Let the Holy Ghost and the Word of God reign in your heart. That's how we diligently guard our hearts. Below a couple of verses that will certainly put things in the right perspective:

- *And He said to them, "Take heed and beware of covetousness, for one's life does not consist in the abundance of the things he possesses (Luke 12:15)."*

- *Set your mind on things above, not on things on the earth (Colossians 3:2).*

- *While we do not look at the things which are seen, but at the things which are not seen. For the things which are seen are temporary, but the things which are not seen are eternal (2 Corinthians 4:18).*

- *For we brought nothing into the world, and we can take nothing out of it (1 Timothy 6:7).*

26. Wealth is To Be Enjoyed

As for every man to whom God has given riches and wealth, and given him power to eat of it, to receive his heritage and rejoice in his labor—this is the gift of God.

Ecclesiastes 5:19

Solomon was the wisest man that has ever lived and one of the wealthiest men who lived up to that time. Tradition says that Ecclesiastes was written by King Solomon in his old age. He focused primarily on earthly life and not spiritual life in Ecclesiastes. By the time he wrote the book of Ecclesiastes, he had accrued a lot of life experience. And wisdom. He probably experienced a lot of ups and downs in his spiritual, (inter)personal, emotional, and financial life. He was a real observer and you know what was one of the greatest evils he had ever seen? Not being able to enjoy riches and wealth.

There is an evil which I have seen under the sun, and it is common among men: A man to whom God has given riches and wealth and honor, so that he lacks nothing for himself of all he desires; yet God does not give him power to eat of it, but a foreigner consumes it. This is vanity, and it is an evil affliction.

Ecclesiastes 6:1-2

Ecclesiastes 5:19 and Ecclesiastes 6:1-2 make one thing very clear: it is a gift of God to be able to enjoy wealth. Referring once again to the rich fool in Luke 12 (verse 16-21). The rich fool gathered a lot and said to himself *"Soul, you have many goods laid up for many years; take your ease; eat, drink, and be merry.* But God did not grant him the enjoyment of this wealth. It is one thing to receive the blessing of wealth, but it is *another blessing* to be able to *enjoy* that wealth.

*Command those who are rich in this present age not to be haughty, nor to trust in uncertain riches but in the living God, **who gives us richly all things to enjoy.***

1 Timothy 6:17

Wealth is to be enjoyed. How can we enjoy wealth? That's up to each individual, but never forget God in it. Here some free tips. Break free from the noise in yourself that keeps on saying the more the better. Learn to relax, be at ease and content with what you have. Learn to count your blessings. Have fun and laugh. Spend your wealth on quality time with your loved ones. Invest your money in experiences rather than only in things and possessions. Share your wealth with your loved ones and the needy. This is true enjoyment! After all, it is more blessed to give than to receive (Acts 20:35)!

27. Wealth is Power

Now there was found in it a poor wise man, and he by his wisdom
delivered the city. Yet no one remembered that same poor man.

Then I said:

"Wisdom is better than strength.
Nevertheless the poor man's wisdom is despised,
And his words are not heard.

Ecclesiastes 9:15-16

King Solomon narrates a story of a poor man that was very wise and delivered the city. Yet no one remembered that man. The Good News Translation even says *"he could have saved"* the town. But no one thought about him. The poor man's wisdom is despised. Wealth is influence, *wealth is power*. Why? I believe because in men's eyes, wealth is generally seen as *a certification of ability*. I believe this was even way more important in Solomon's society where degrees and grades were of no (or little) importance. Even in today's world where degrees and grades certify man's ability, money still says a lot in society's eyes about who to take seriously.

> *Wealth makes many friends,*
> *But the poor is separated from his friend.*

Proverbs 19:4

Wealth makes friends. Jesus also encourages us to make friends through money (Luke 16:9). This means that wealth can give an ability to have influence. The Bible also says the rich rule over the poor (Proverbs 22:7). I believe this does not have to do with spiritual power but with power in society.

So, through the Word of God we learn that wealth has to do with power:

- *Wealth can add weight to words which in essence is power of influence*

- *Wealth gives influence through expansion of a network*

- *Wealth is power through positions as wealth can simplify access to positions of rulership*

Does that mean that we as Christians should use wealth to force ourselves into positions of influence? No, not at all. In no means am I talking about *forcing* stuff with money. We should not want to gain positions of influence through financial malpractices (like bribery; Proverbs 15:27).

The message that I am trying to convey is that with wealth power comes, if you like it or not. It is like an automatic mechanism that is activated in this world as soon as wealth increases and we should be aware of it. People automatically look at you (or look up to you) in one way or the other when you are wealthy. This isn't something that should surprise us as it is something that goes back in time and I believe it will never change. Due to wealth, one is also treated differently and a certain responsibility comes with it. How we respond to this attention shows our heart condition. We should be prepared for certain positions of influence and never misuse power.

The Bible warns that a position of wealth in no way gives the right to extort the poor (Proverbs 21:13, Proverbs 22:16, Proverbs 22:22-23) nor should we show partiality (also see James 2). In addition, in no way we are encouraged to reach a state of wealth just to take in power. However, when power is used positively, of course this is a nice side effect to wealth.

As worthy stewards of God, I pray that we will use our wealth and the power that comes with it, in a proper way so we will expand God's Kingdom.

28. Wealth Brings Responsibility

*For everyone to whom much is given, from him much will be
required; and to whom much has been committed, of him they will
ask the more.*

Luke 12:48b

To whom much is given much is required. Much more is required from the person to whom much more is given. What does this actually mean? I believe it to mean:

Great power gives great responsibility, even greater power gives even greater responsibility.

Deep words. These words are directed to us as Christians. These well-known words were spoken by Jesus after telling the story of an unjust steward that was severely punished after misusing the great power he received in absence of his master. Jesus, our Master, has also entrusted us as Christians with a lot. These words are to be taken in serious consideration by each servant of Christ.

What have we been entrusted with? It's an understatement to say we have been entrusted with a lot: the knowledge of Him, His Word and the mysteries that have been hidden for centuries (Romans 16:25,26; 1 Corinthians 2:7-10), the Holy Ghost (Ephesians 1:13-14), the power to heal the sick, cast out devils and perform signs, miracles and wonders in His name (Mark 16:16-18), the inheritance of Christ (Romans 8:17), and the Great Commission (Matthew 28:18-20), to name a few. But also in line with the parables, He gave us gifts and talents.

He gave us these gifts and talents and we ought to use them. Use them to multiply and further the Kingdom. He is also the One that gives us wealth. It works in more ways, as we have seen that wealth is power. Remember, great power is great responsibility.

Wealth gives us responsibility in more ways:

- *Responsibility to honor God with it (Proverbs 3:9)*

- *Responsibility to support God's ministers (1 Timothy 5:18)*

- *Responsibility to support Kingdom expansion with it (Matthew 6:21; Matthew 6:33)*

- *Responsibility to take care of our family financially (1 Timothy 5:8)*

- *Responsibility to take care of the needy (Proverbs 28:27)*

- *Responsibility to manage our hearts and character properly (Psalm 62:10)*

All these responsibilities apply to every Christian but *the more you have, the greater your responsibility, also in giving (Deuteronomy 16:17).* God keeps an eye on our giving (Matthew 10:42; Mark 12:41)!

Remember that before the unjust steward the faithful steward is mentioned. Keep in mind that the faithful steward, the one that used his greater power in a responsible way, was greatly rewarded and use this lesson as a life goal!

29. Wealth is Protection

*For wisdom is a defense as **money is a defense**,*
But the excellence of knowledge is that wisdom gives life to those
who have it.

Ecclesiastes 7:12

In Hebrew, the word *shadow* is used in Ecclesiastes 7:12 instead of *defense*. It's clear to see that a shadow is a defense by providing protection against a scorching sun. Other translations say money is a shelter. A shelter is a place giving us temporary protection from bad weather or danger. A buffer of money protects us from the stormy financial seasons in our lives. Note that the wise always save up (Proverbs 21:20).

The rich rules over the poor,
And the borrower is servant to the lender.

Proverbs 22:7

If it's hard to picture money as security, let's envision the opposite: lack of money. The lack of money oftentimes means borrowing which brings you in a situation of restraint. For some people, money represents freedom — money gives them the freedom to do as they please, and *not* having money (or worse, being in debt) constrains them. In situations where we're unable to pay due to a lack of finances, our stuff can be taken or even worse our house (Proverbs 22:26-27). Being wealthy can mean an avoidance of these practices. Not having money implies that at any given moment our lives could come crashing down.

God is *the* defense and is always *our* ultimate security. But realize that money is a defense and may provide us with (some degree of) security. I want to conclude by paraphrasing the Bible commentator Jarchi: *He that is in the shadow of wisdom often also sits in the shadow of money, for wisdom is one of the causes why riches come.*

30. Wealth Can Be Used For Worship

But I have received everything in full and more; I am amply supplied, having received from Epaphroditus the gifts you sent me. They are the fragrant aroma of an offering, an acceptable sacrifice which God welcomes and in which He delights.

Philippians 4:18

Firstly, we should give *ourselves* as living sacrifices to God as an act of worship (Romans 12:1 AMP). Secondly, giving *our wealth* back to God is also seen as an act of worship. We know that we can honor Him with our possessions (Proverbs 3:9). But the Bible also declares we can *worship* Him with our offering. The Church in Philippi gave financial gifts to Paul. Paul compares these financial gifts to the fragrant aroma of an offering that was presented to God.

Worship is defined as a feeling or expression of reverence and adoration. Under the Law of Moses, there were several offerings presented to God: burnt offerings, grain offerings, drink offerings etc.

These were all a shadow of the things to come, and have all been put away by the ultimate offering of Christ on the cross. But all these instructions reveal to us a simple fact: *offering matters to God*. But how to give offerings worshipfully to God?

I believe that to give *worshipfully* means giving voluntary, purposefully, cheerfully and not grudgingly (2 Corinthians 9:5-7). And remember: the more you have, the greater your responsibility. So if you're wealthy the more you should worship God out of your position of wealth.

Many times as a young man I just ran off to Church just before the service started. Once it was offering time I would reach out to my pockets and gave God the coins I could find there. Sometimes my pockets were empty. This was not reverent at all!

In my defense, I have always been a big fan of digital payments, so I didn't typically carry cash money with me wherever I went. Thank God for the technological advances in our societies and churches where nowadays we can easily transfer money by our smartphones or by using our debit cards. However, digital payment methods do not exempt us from overthinking our offering. Heedless giving is no worship either!

How many times have we stood in God's House and when it was offering time we just reached into our pockets or our wallets to "just give Him something". We should really ask Him for forgiveness for all the times we *just gave* Him an offering.

I think one of the other keys of giving worshipfully is giving sacrificially. David insisted on paying for a field that was offered to him for free, as he did not want to give God anything that he received for free. He delivered a true act of worship!

> *Therefore by Him let us continually offer the sacrifice of praise to God, that is, the fruit of our lips, giving thanks to His name. But do not forget to do good and to share, **for with such sacrifices God is well pleased.***

> *Hebrews 13:15-16*

Worship Him with your wealth and never forget to share with others. These premises exemplify a well-pleasing act of worship to God.

31. Money Should Be A Servant, Not A Master

"No one can serve two masters; for either he will hate the one and love the other, or he will be devoted to the one and despise the other. You cannot serve God and mammon [money, possessions, fame, status, or whatever is valued more than the Lord].

Matthew 6:24 AMP

No one can serve two *masters*. It's God or money. We need to choose. It's not only about choosing with our *mouth* but with our *hearts*.

What do you mean? The key is found in Matthew 6:24 itself: whatever we love the most or are the most devoted to, is our true master.

We might give lip service on what our true master is but what does our heart say? And as actions speak louder than words, what do our actions say? Anything you give more precious attention than God can become your master.

When British 10 years old were asked in a 2014 survey what they wanted to become when they grow up, 22% answered *rich* and 19% answered *famous (SOURCE: TELEGRAPH UK)*. I am sure that many (young) adults have the same outlook on life: I just want to be rich, no matter what. Becoming rich is the ultimate goal in many lives. I believe this to be a major opening for being enslaved. Many think: whatever makes me rich, I will do. Sounds a lot like: "Master, whatever you say, I will do." Right?

It's the same for those that hate their jobs from the bottom of their hearts but still keep on doing it for years as if they were slaves without any right to "escape".

Don't think money does everything or you are going to end up doing everything for money. – Voltaire

Questions to ask yourself to check whether money is your master:

- *A master is someone you lay your own principles aside for; do you lay aside God's principles for money?*
- *Do you lay aside your personal core values for money?*
- *A master is someone you listen to even over your own well-being; do you forsake your own well-being (health) for money?*

So, how can we let money serve us?

Remember the rule, that money should be attracted and not pursued? Well, put it into practice. A servant follows a master not the other way around, right?

If we command our wealth, we shall be rich and free. If our wealth commands us, we are poor indeed. —Edmund Burke

32. God's Prosperity is Not Dependent on the World's Economy

Blessed is the man who trusts in the Lord,
And whose hope is the Lord.
For he shall be like a tree planted by the waters,
Which spreads out its roots by the river,
And will not fear when heat comes;
But its leaf will be green,
And will not be anxious in the year of drought,
Nor will cease from yielding fruit.

Jeremiah 17:7-8

By the grace of God, I earned a university degree in economics. In economics, it is known that the economy goes up and down in cycles. But we are not to trust only in man's system. In fact, we are cursed if we do (Jeremiah 17:5). If we trust in the Lord, we are like a tree planted by the waters that will never cease from yielding fruit *even in the year of drought (Jeremiah 17:8).*

> *A thousand may fall at your side,*
>
> *And ten thousand at your right hand;*
>
> *But it shall not come near you.*

Psalm 91:7

Psalm 91 is one of the most popular psalms. Even the Devil quoted it (Matthew 4:6)! Its promises of protection are marvelous. A thousand may fall on our side, and ten thousand at our right side but we will not be harmed. *Why? Because you have made the Lord, the most High God, your refuge and your dwelling place (Psalm 91:9).*

He is the One we need to look up to in times of drought. He is the One that promises us protection even though danger is all around us. Remember what happened when Isaac wanted to flee from a famine?

Then the Lord appeared to him and said: *"Do not go down to Egypt; live in the land of which I shall tell you. **Dwell in this land, and I will be with you and bless you (Genesis 26:2-3).***

Even in unfavorable economic times, He favored Isaac and fed him. The earth is the Lord's and the fulness thereof (Psalm 24:1 KJV). The Creator of heaven and earth is not restricted by any circumstance. Remember He has the ability to lead you to places where you have access to immeasurable sources (Luke 5:4-8). He will never leave nor forsake us, He will strengthen, help and uphold us (Deuteronomy 31:6; Isaiah 41:10-13) and push us forward *even in times of drought.*

33. Money Can't Buy Everything

And when Simon saw that through the laying on of the apostles'
hands the Holy Spirit was given, he offered them money, saying,
"Give me this power also, that anyone on whom I lay hands may
receive the Holy Spirit."

But Peter said to him, "Your money perish with you, because you
thought that the gift of God could be purchased with money!

Acts 8:18-20

The story of Peter and Simon the sorcerer illustrates one thing: money can't buy everything. God's gifts, for example, are not for sale. We all probably know the saying that money can't buy happiness. Solomon already knew about this truth. The Bible tells us that one of the evils King Solomon saw is that some received the gift of wealth but could never enjoy it (Ecclesiastes 6:1-2). Money just doesn't have the ability to buy us joy or happiness.

For what profit is it to a man if he gains the whole world, and loses his own soul? Or what will a man give in exchange for his soul (Matthew 16:26)?

We could own the whole world but what can we offer God in exchange for our souls? *Absolutely nothing.* We can never buy our way to heaven. The price of heaven cannot be expressed in material terms.

Here a list of other important things money can't buy:

- *Freedom*

- *Peace (of mind)*

- *Good health*

- *Ultimate security*

- *Grace*

- *Love*

Money is very important in life and even in God's Kingdom. But for all these things we should go to God. I do not expect that this point will create a lot of "wait, what moments" but this is just meant to put things into perspective. If we only focus on the good and positive things concerning wealth and don't present the counterview that the Bible also has to offer, nothing more than a false image is created.

By covering all the Bible has to say on wealth a complete picture is shown. Of course, through the means of money you can get a lot done. However, money can't buy everything and can't get everything done. Please let this sink into your heart to be able to see money and wealth in the right perspective.

34. Wealth Should Be Invested Wisely

Cast your bread upon the waters,

For you will find it after many days.

Give a serving to seven, and also to eight,

For you do not know what evil will be on the earth.

Ecclesiastes 11:1-2

King Solomon, one of the wealthiest persons that has ever lived (if not the wealthiest), sure had a lot of wise insights concerning wealth. Solomon basically says, in Ecclesiastes 11:1-2, to not lay all eggs in one basket. This saying of the wise means that one should not concentrate all efforts and resources in one area as there always lies a danger in the basket hitting the ground resulting in losing everything at once. We don't know and never completely will, what evil will be on the earth, so when possible, it's always a good strategy to reduce risk.

Is Solomon's advice still applicable in modern days? Yes. According to several investing experts, it still is. In investing terminology, it's called *diversification*. Solomon advises to invest wisely and diversifying by spreading risk over seven, even eight areas.

What is the bread Solomon is referring to in Ecclesiastes 11:1? Is it only our money? No, I believe it to stand for our *resources*, which is a broader term. Thus, I believe it also to express our time and our labor.

You know, one of the key investing tools of the average human being is putting money in a bank account and accumulating interest. Just recently (at the time of writing it is the end of 2019), I looked at the average interest rate. In Europe (the Netherlands) the average interest rate on a savings account is around 0,02%. So, EUR 1.000 or USD 1.000 after a year makes 20 cents. So, by placing my money on a bank account and waiting for interest, I'm almost starting to feel like the lazy worthless servant that just hid his talent into the ground!

Another resource is our labor. For many of us, labor or work is our only strategy to extract money from, making us able to pay the bill. But what if we get laid off? Only relying on our job for income is not a wise strategy. The Bible advises us to have 7 or even 8 areas where we can get money from.

Have you ever considered, for example, investing in:

- *Gold, silver or other precious metals?*
- *Real estate?*
- *Stocks?*
- *Promising start-up companies?*
- *Promising upcoming industries?*

- *Cryptocurrencies*

Let's ask our Lord for wisdom and insight so we will not miss all the opportunities presented to us to invest wisely! Remember to cast out fear!

35. Wealth Through Sacrifice for God's Kingdom

Then Peter began to say to Him, "See, we have left all and followed You."

So Jesus answered and said, "Assuredly, I say to you, there is no one who has left house or brothers or sisters or father or mother or wife or children or lands, for My sake and the gospel's, who shall not receive a hundredfold now in this time—houses and brothers and sisters and mothers and children and lands, with persecutions—and in the age to come, eternal life.

Mark 10:28-30

Concerning the topic of wealth in the Bible, there are many misconceptions, especially concerning the New Testament's stance on wealth. There are some Christians who adhere to the belief that the Bible says that money is evil. I think there are especially two Scripture parts that are misquoted by "the money is evil group". Firstly, people frequently misquote the Bible by insisting the Bible says "Money is the root of all evil". But that's not what the Bible actually says. 1 Timothy 6:10 reveals that the *love of* money is the root of all evil". A big and crucial difference. Money is just a tool and has no heart. It's about the hearts of people in relation to money.

Rich young ruler

The story of the rich young ruler is another part of Scripture that is typically used by people to say "you see, money is evil, we should get rid of it to follow Jesus!". But, I believe the story to be wrongly understood. Mark 10:17-22 accounts the story of a rich young ruler that was God-fearing. However, when the rich young ruler was asked by Jesus to sell all his possessions and follow Him, the Bible records that the young man became sad and went away "for he had great possessions". Then Jesus confirms how it's very hard for those that trust in and have riches to enter the Kingdom of God. He also says:

It is easier for a camel to go through the eye of a needle, than for a rich man to enter into the Kingdom of God.

How can a camel go through the eye of a needle? Impossible! I believe this to be a strong metaphor of Jesus. In the wall of the old Jerusalem, there was a great big iron gate which was closed every night. In principle, that gate was never to be opened before sunrise the next day. However, it would sometimes happen that a traveler on a camel would arrive at the gate after dark, seeking to be admitted into the city. When this happened, a small gate inside the main iron gate was opened. The man seeking entrance would come of his camel, strip the camel of everything on its back, urge the camel to its knees and then, with great difficulty, the camel could just barely squeeze through. Do you know what the name was of that small gate? It was known as *the Eye of the*

Needle.

I like how the great Bible teacher Derek Prince explains it:

In His response to the rich young ruler, Jesus was describing how it is when a rich man comes to the kingdom of God. He has to lay aside all of his baggage—all his pretension, pride, arrogance, independence—and get down on his knees in order to just barely squeeze through. However, a poor man who carries nothing in his hand but a staff can get through much more easily. All he has to do is stoop, pass through and he is on the inside. The same gate is for all, whether rich or poor. But so often it is harder for the rich to get through than it is for the poor.

So that puts the impossibility of a rich man entering heaven in a whole other perspective right? Plus, Jesus says that with God all things are possible. But even though it's possible, should we get rid of our possessions first to follow Him?

No, not always. Jesus can see through our hearts and saw that in the rich young ruler's case it was a hindrance. But let's see what else the Bible says.

> *Then Peter began to say to Him, "See, we have left all and followed You."*
>
> *So Jesus answered and said, "Assuredly, I say to you, there is no one who has left house or brothers or sisters or father or mother or wife or children or lands, for My sake and the gospel's, who shall not receive a hundredfold **now in this time**—**houses** and brothers and sisters and mothers and children and **lands**, with persecutions—and in the age to come, eternal life (Mark 10:28-29).*

So, if we sacrifice matters for the Kingdom, He will repay us. When? *Now in this time*. With what? Only spiritual things? No, also material: *houses and lands* (or fields). And multiplied (a hundredfold)! So if wealth and possessions equate to something evil why would Jesus repay us with these things abundantly?

Through sacrifice, wealth comes. Take comfort in the fact that the Bible says that when we sacrifice things to follow Him, He will never forget this and will repay us abundantly in this time *and* in the age to come!

36. Wealth Can Be Deceitful

*Now he who received seed among the thorns is he who hears the word, and the cares of this world and **the deceitfulness of riches** choke the word, and he becomes unfruitful.*

Matthew 13:22

oney talks. And it tells a lot of lies too. One of the most popular parables of Jesus is the parable of the Sower. In this parable, a sower goes out to sow seed. Some seed fell by the wayside, some on stony places, some among thorns and some in good ground. The seed stands for the Word of the Kingdom, the Gospel, and how it enters people's hearts. Now, look what the parable says about the seed that falls among the thorns. The Word is choked by the cares of this world and *the deceitfulness of riches.*

Riches or wealth can be deceitful. Another word for deceitful is misleading. Like Paul states: through the covetous pursuit of riches many fall into temptation and a snare, and into many foolish and hurtful lusts, which drown men in destruction and perdition. Through the covetous pursuit of money, many lose the faith and pierce themselves through with many sorrows (1 Timothy 6:9-10).

What are some of the deceitful things riches convey?

1. Once you have me, you don't need God anymore.

2. Once you have me, you don't need others.

3. Once you have me, you're free of any responsibility. You can just do what you want.

4. Once you have me, you're worth more than others.

5. Once you have me, you will be happy

None other than Satan, the father of lies (John 8:44), tells us the same things. Basically, it says seek ye first money and everything shall follow. *Remember, we should have money. Money should not have us.*

We should never think that we are immune for the deceitfulness of riches. Let him who thinks he stands take heed lest he fall (1 Corinthians 10:12). Be on your guard against all kinds of greed (Luke 12:15). We should keep on asking God for a sincere, mature and pure heart to handle our wealth and to remain humble. Then riches are not able to deceive us and can only be a blessing!

37. Wealth in Contentment

*I know how to get along and live humbly [in difficult times], and I
also know how to enjoy abundance and live in prosperity. In any
and every circumstance I have learned the secret [of facing life],
whether well-fed or going hungry, whether having an abundance or
being in need.*

Philippians 4:12 AMP

The New King James Version Translation says in Philippians
4:11: *"I have learned in whatever state I am, to be content."* Being
content is defined as being in a state of happiness and
satisfaction. *There should be contentment in wealth but there should also be
wealth in contentment.* Contentment in wealth as the Bible teaches us
that the *enjoyment of wealth* is a gift of God (Ecclesiastes 5:19), so this
should bring us into that state of happiness and satisfaction. Yet,
mastering contentment itself (without looking at our financial state) is
also a possession of great value. The Bible teaches us that no matter
what kind of financial state we find ourselves in, we should learn to be
content.

Now godliness with contentment is great gain [that contentment which comes from a sense of inner confidence based on the sufficiency of God].

1 Timothy 6:6 AMP

How can contentment be great gain or wealth for us that live godly? The Amplified Bible says that it is great gain when it is that contentment which comes from *a sense of inner confidence* based on the sufficiency of God. Yet, I would like to rephrase that and say that *contentment which comes from **faith** in the sufficiency of God is great gain.*

Being content teaches us about faith. The faith that knows God will provide us with what we need. It teaches us to rely on Him. After rain fair weather comes. Being content, no matter what, forms our character. It's a test for us. As a matter of fact, besides faith, I believe contentment has a direct link with all the other attributes of the fruit of the Spirit (Galatians 5:22-23). Faith is also sometimes translated as faithfulness in Galatians 5:22. Shouldn't we all strive to practice the attributes of the fruit of the Spirit in our lives?

- Love – we can unselfishly care for others, as we are content with what we have, we are easily willing to help others

- Joy – contentment is a state of joy and satisfaction

- Peace – no matter what our bank account says, we may experience peace as we know that it's just for a season and God will ultimately provide

- Longsuffering or patience – contentment gives us the

ability to patiently trust in God and His outworking. Etc. etc.

I can do all things by Christ who strengthens me (Philippians 4:13) is one of the most popular Bible verses from which power is derived. Keep in mind that this verse comes after Paul says he can get by no matter what his financial situation may look like. There is wealth in contentment. I believe that, ultimately, if we hold fast to His promises and walk in line with His Word, we cannot remain in a financial dry season for long. *And my God shall supply all your need according to His riches in glory by Christ Jesus (Philippians 4:19)!*

38. *Wealth Should Not Be Loved*

For the love of money is a root of all kinds of evil, for which some have strayed from the faith in their greediness, and pierced themselves through with many sorrows.

1 Timothy 6:10

As already mentioned, 1 Timothy 6:10 is one of the most misquoted verses of the Bible, particularly for those who adhere to the belief that money is evil. Note that the Bible does not say that money is a root of all kinds of evil. It says THE LOVE OF MONEY. *Money (wealth) is as good or bad as what one does with it.* It is about the hearts of people in relation to money.

The Amplified Bible says: *For the love of money [that is, the greedy desire for it and the willingness to gain it unethically] is a root of all sorts of evil, and some by longing for it have wandered away from the faith and pierced themselves [through and through] with many sorrows.*

The love of money is the greedy desire for it and the willingness to gain it unethically. What goes on in our hearts concerning money? As Christians, we are exhorted to examine ourselves continually (1

Corinthians 11:28, 2 Corinthians 13:5). Below are a few relevant questions to self-examine our hearts in relation to money:

- *Is money the most important factor driving you in undertaking certain actions or in decision making?*

- *Is accumulating money your main goal in life?*

- *What's the reason that you desire an abundance of money? Study James 4*

- *Do you perform actions with the sole intent of making money?*

- *Does your day primarily revolve around making money (by any means)?*

- *Are you willing to disobey God and lay aside His Word for money?*

- *Are you willing to lay aside your personal core values for money?*

- *Do you notice less willingness to perform certain actions when less or no money is involved with it, or do you execute these actions with excellence? Remember: whatsoever you do, do it with passion, as for the Lord and not for people (Colossians 3:23)*

Sincerely answering the above questions will expose whether covetousness or greed has a place in our hearts.

Greed is a sin against God, just as all mortal sins, in as much as man condemns things eternal for the sake of temporal things. – Theologian Thomas Aquinas

In essence, what the Bible says is that love of money is equal to (extreme) greed. An unhealthy obsession for money. Remember that the Bible says that love is as strong as death (Song of Solomon 8:6).

I remember a bold preacher's (that liked using statements with a controversial edge to awaken his hearers) funny statement: I don't LOVE money, I LIKE money. Somewhat a funny and bold statement. As there is a crucial difference between liking and loving (also in the biblical sense), the statement does contain truth. Are we (unknowingly) enslaved by money? We should continually self-examine our hearts. Let's end in prayer:

Lord, You are our number one love. There is nothing that can replace You. We ask You to cleanse us completely from any covetousness or greed that may reside in our hearts. Please reveal all things in our hearts that don't belong there. Teach us to be content and to trust in your abundant provision. Good Father, we thank You for all You have given us and what You will continue to give us. Amen.

39. Lack is Not Pretty

The rich man's wealth is his strong city;
The destruction of the poor is their poverty.

Proverbs 10:15

Poverty, in the end, will lead to destruction. The Bible says that Satan came to steal, kill and destroy (John 10:10). Job, for example, went through a season of poverty and I'm sure Paul also experienced rough financial seasons (remember God causes all things to work together for good for those who love Him, Romans 8:28 AMP, so it might be a lesson from Him). I sincerely believe, however, that living in poverty *continually*, from the cradle to the grave, is not of God and is nothing more than the enemy's plan.

Poverty is not easy to define as it is a relative term. When is someone actually poor? Should we use western standards? Should we use minimum wage as demarcation? That's why I prefer to use the term *lack* which is easier to picture. I would define poverty as being in lack (of basic needs).

> *The Lord is my shepherd;*
>
> *I shall not want.*
>
> *Psalm 23:1*

I shall not want, the literal translation says *I shall not lack*. Lack is the state of not having (enough of) something. Some Christians believe that wealth is something to be avoided and worldly possessions shouldn't be gathered and enjoyed. But is lack (and learning to deal with it) something that shows someone's great religious or spiritual level? Some Christians would answer this question with a loud "yes".

I believe it is truly admirable and praiseworthy, and also well-pleasing in God's eyes, when someone is able to serve God wholeheartedly *despite* a difficult financial situation. Remember the poor widow (Mark 12:41-44) that was praised by Jesus? A special kind of humility can be found in many of those that do not have a lot, which is to be cherished. The rich are often more likely to be puffed up (James 5:1-6; 1 Timothy 6:17). But is the lack of finances in itself pretty and something we as believers should seek? Absolutely not. Apart from humbling us, which we as Christians are encouraged to do no matter what (1 Peter 5:5), lack is not pretty at all.

The lack of basic needs is not pretty. It really gets a face in Deuteronomy 28. And it's not a pretty face. No housing, no clothing, no food. In one word: misery. But look at all the blessings mentioned in Deuteronomy 28 linked to obedience: blessings that impact basically every area of our lives. Isn't this something we should strive for?

Do you really think that God want us to remain in a state where we don't have enough food for ourselves and our children? Does God want us to struggle with simple bills for basic needs (light and water bills etc.) our entire lives on earth? Absolutely not. If those that are evil know how to give good gifts to their children, how much more Our Father (Matthew 7:11)?

I believe dealing with poverty from the cradle to the grave is nothing more than a (generational) curse (see for example the curses for disobedience in Deuteronomy 28). The spirit of poverty is like a haunting spirit that can go on from generation to generation, affecting multiple lives physically, mentally and spiritually. Sometimes you meet very talented people and you wonder why they still live in lack. It is as if the spirit of poverty has bound them and covered their eyes from seeing their potential (didn't their parents and grandparents also struggle? So their situation is "normal"). Their way of thinking is affected and oozes the "poor man's mentality (which I believe to be inheritable)". Besides passing on the "poor man's mentality", do you know that even debts can be inherited? But Jesus has given us power to break any curse! Our intention must be to only leave *positive* inheritances for our offspring.

According to Solomon, being rich (and righteous, Proverbs 28:6) is to be preferred over being poor (Proverbs 10:15; Proverbs 14:20; Proverbs 19:4; Proverbs 19:6-7; Proverbs 22:7). Keep in mind however, that being poor does not mean that one does not walk with God. We should never show favor towards people based on their bank accounts (see James 4). Remember, faith and righteousness are not merely the only thing that lead to riches.

I believe that once we follow God and His principles, we will come to a place where we will not lack and struggle from paycheck to paycheck. I believe that God does not want us to live a life of lack. Remember, His eye is even on the sparrow. He cares about us and our financial situation. Cast out that way of thinking that says "ah well, maybe God just wants me to live this life of lack on earth, I'm just happy to be saved, in heaven all will be well".

Of course, Jesus' gift of salvation is not to be compared with any material thing but never close your mind for all the marvelous things He can do on the level of material blessings. Actively pursue His blessings. He is able to supply *all* our needs according to His riches in glory by Christ Jesus (Philippians 4:19). Keep in mind you can be *and* saved *and* financially blessed!

40. Wealth-Handling Shows Love

I speak not by commandment, but I am testing the sincerity of your love by the diligence of others.

2 Corinthians 8:8

God is love. Whoever does not love does not know God, because God is love (1 John 4:8). The greatest thing is love (1 Corinthians 13:13). Are wealth and love connected? Yes, certainly. Through your handling of wealth, your love is expressed. Another crucial thing in wealth-handling is *proportionality*.

I will explain two principles by using a simple example. Let's say you have hit the jackpot business-wise which means you don't have to worry about money at all. To celebrate your wife's birthday (or your special marriage anniversary) you buy your wife flowers or a box of chocolate. Women sure love flowers and chocolate as gifts, right? However, will she be happy with your gift? I doubt it. It is not about the (value of the) gift but the fact that your wife knows you have enough money (as she sees you spending a lot of your fortune on other insignificant things) but you did not spend it on her. What we give should be *in proportion* to our wealth (1 Corinthians 16:2) as this shows our love.

So, I have just mentioned two principles that are important for wealth-handling in relation to love:

1. *Your wealth is directed to the things you love*

For where your treasure is, there your heart will also be (Luke 12:34); which means (among other things) where your money is, there is your love.

"Don't tell me where your priorities are. Show me where you spend your money and I'll tell you what they are." —James W. Frick

2. *The law of proportionality*

We're always encouraged to give in proportion. It is not about the amount we give, but the proportion to what we have. For example, the poor widow that gave all she had was praised (Mark 12:41-44). The principle of tithing endorses the same law.

When God blesses you financially do not (only) raise your standard of living. Raise your standard of giving. – Mark Batterson

How we handle our wealth shows our love *for* God and our love *of* God (1 John 3:18). Giving to God is honoring Him as the giver and loving Him for who He is and what He has done. Paul says to the Corinthians that the sincerity of our Godly love is shown towards others through the handling of our finances (2 Corinthians 8:8). But, always remember to give out of love! If given out of guilt, obligation or for boastful purposes, you may miss blessings (1 Corinthians 13:3). Apart from, 2 Corinthians 8:8, other Bible verses show the same principle of expressing love through the handling of finances:

> *My little children, let us not love in word or in tongue, but in deed and in truth.*

> *1 John 3:18*

Faith without works is dead. I would like to add that *love* without works is also dead. We should love *in deed* (in other words, in works) and in truth. Do you know which deed is used as an example? The deed of helping others with our finances:

> *But whoever has this world's goods, and sees his brother in need, and shuts up his heart from him, how does the love of God abide in him?*

> *1 John 3:17*

In other words, how we handle our wealth shows our love. It speaks to the one that *has this world's goods*, a nice way of saying, the one that is rich *(see for example the NIV translation)*. Remember, the greatest love ever displayed was also shown by action (John 3:16; Ephesians 5:1-2). I encourage us all to handle our finances with love, in love and to show our love through it.

You can give without loving, but you cannot love without giving – Amy Carmichael

41. Wealth Should Be Acquired Honestly and Ethically

"You shall not have in your bag differing weights, a heavy and a light. You shall not have in your house differing measures, a large and a small. You shall have a perfect and just weight, a perfect and just measure, that your days may be lengthened in the land which the Lord your God is giving you. For all who do such things, all who behave unrighteously, are an abomination to the Lord your God.

Deuteronomy 25:13-16

In ancient Israel, several measurement units were used for trade. For precious metals, for example, two scales were used and the weight of the goods to sell was derived from a stone that traders carried in their bag. Fraudsters had different swindling tactics. For example, fraudsters that wanted to buy precious metals would carry a stone that was too light, so they would get more than required compared to when the correct measuring stone was used. Fraudsters that wanted to sell, on the other hand, would use a heavier stone to give less than was actually required in comparison to when the correct measuring stone was used. These dishonest practices in doing business were nothing more than an abomination to the Lord.

> Wealth gained by dishonesty will be diminished,
> But he who gathers by labor will increase.

Proverbs 13:11

Nowadays most multinational companies, if not all, try to conduct business in line with Corporate Social Responsibility. Corporate Social Responsibility (also called corporate sustainability, corporate conscience, conscious capitalism or responsible business) is simply said a business concept whereby companies take into account the well-being of society and the environment. Companies not involved in CSR will definitely catch negative public attention which eventually will be felt in their finances.

It should be no surprise that the Bible has a lot to say about doing business in a socially responsible and ethical manner. Let's look at some of the things that can be found in the Bible concerning doing business and acquiring wealth:

1. We should always conduct business in a fair and ethical way

We should always conduct business in a fair and ethical way. This message should come as no surprise. Lying is a sin and God hates dishonest practices (Proverbs 12:22). In fact, wealth gained by dishonesty will be diminished (Proverbs 13:11). The lives of those that are involved in fair conduct however, will be blessed (Deuteronomy 25:15).

2. Employees should be treated fairly

> *Indeed the wages of the laborers who mowed your fields, which you kept back by fraud, cry out; and the cries of the reapers have reached the ears of the Lord of Sabaoth.*

> *James 5:4*

Employers have the social responsibility to treat their employees well. Remember that their cries may end up in the ears of God. Even slave masters were encouraged to treat their slaves justly and fair (Colossians 4:1) as we all have a Master in heaven.

3. We should take care of the environment

> *The Lord God took the man and put him in the Garden of Eden to work it and take care of it*

> *Genesis 2:15 NIV*

Adam was told to work in the garden of Eden and to take care of it. Not to damage it, or do with it whatever he wanted. In essence, he was instructed to take care of it. It was God who created our planet (Genesis 1:1) and He placed us to live on His creation. Following the principle of stewardship, should we not steward His creation in the most caring way?

The Bible says that the righteous take care of the needs of their animals (Proverbs 12:10). In addition, should we not leave a great inheritance for our children, including planet Earth (Proverbs 13:22)? Any practice involving wealth creation while heavily damaging God's creation and gift should be thought over carefully.

In business, there is a popular saying, "the customer is king". Jesus said: "Treat others the same way you want them to treat you" (Luke 6:31). Wouldn't you want to be treated as a king or queen? If we would follow this rule in business, wouldn't the business environment (and the world for that matter) be a far nicer place? Don't go at any length for wealth. It's the greedy desire for money and the willingness to gain it unethically that's the root of all sorts of evil (1 Timothy 6:10). Be encouraged to acquire wealth in an honest and ethical way that is in line with God's will.

42. Wealth Through Excellence

*He has **unusual ability** and is wise and skillful in interpreting dreams, solving riddles, and explaining mysteries; so send for this man Daniel, whom the king named Belteshazzar, and he will tell you what all this means."*

Daniel 5:12

The book of Daniel tells the story of Daniel, a God-fearing young man who was taken into captivity by Babylonians. After remaining faithful to God through all circumstances, Daniel rose to power. As a high-ranking person in Babylonia, Daniel was also wealthy and prosperous (Daniel 5:29; 6:28); One of his keys to wealth? The Bible says that Daniel had *unusual ability (Daniel 5:12)*. Other Bible translations say that he had *an excellent spirit*. For the word "excellence", the Hebrew word *yattir* is used. This can also be translated as *exceedingly, extraordinary* or *exceptional*. Being excellent in the things you do is more than "just being good".

Daniel distinguished himself above the governors and satraps because an excellent spirit was in him (Daniel 6:3) or as is said in other translations, because he possessed exceptional qualities. Showcasing our exceptional qualities will distinguish ourselves in the marketplace. Excellence will distinguish you from all the others in the marketplace that are "just" good in their work. As you strive to deliver *extraordinary* work you *will* stand out and this will undoubtedly attract wealth.

Do you see a man who **excels** *in his work?*
He will stand before kings;
He will not stand before unknown men.

Proverbs 22:29

Solomon knew: excellence will bring you before kings. Solomon himself looked out for (extraordinarily) skillful men to build the temple (2 Chronicles 2:7) and I'm sure these skillful men were greatly rewarded. David, Solomon's father knew the same principle as he was brought before King Saul as he was an excellent musician (1 Samuel 16:16-21). Excellence will bring results. I believe that when we combine our God-given talent with hard work and consistency we will manifest God's excellence to the world.

We all have received a certain talent. But we need to polish and sharpen it to make it shine. Whether it is singing, drawing, cooking or writing. During the writing of this book, I more than ever realize that writing is a skill that can be developed. Every skill we execute with consistency will become better by time. When we do our things in excellence time after time, that's when our gifts will prosper us and bring us before great men and women.

Brothers and sisters, in every work that we do, we are encouraged to do it as unto God (Colossians 3:23). If we need to do it like unto Him, shouldn't we always strive to do it in excellence? Cultivate and use the excellence in you and you will be greatly rewarded!

43. Wealth Management Advice: Be Careful with Debt

Owe no one anything except to love one another, for he who loves another has fulfilled the law.

Romans 13:8

The NIV Translation says: *Let no debt remain outstanding, except the continuing debt to love one another, for whoever loves others has fulfilled the law* (Romans 13:8). The Bible never calls borrowing money a sin but does encourage us to avoid debt. In the New and the Old Testament, the same principle is spread out: *be careful with debt.*

There are several reasons to be careful with debt:

1. Debt restricts your freedom

The rich rules over the poor,
And the borrower is servant to the lender.

Proverbs 22:7

Whether it is technically someone in your circle of loved ones or a company: if you borrow you're a servant to the lender. How? You are not truly free in your spending choices anymore as soon as you borrow. In that sense, the lenders have a say in your life. Debt restricts your freedom. When you are unable to pay lenders, the lenders might even have the right to take possessions from you (Proverbs 22:26-27).

2. Debt is often unneeded

"You shall not covet your neighbor's house; you shall not covet your neighbor's wife, nor his male servant, nor his female servant, nor his ox, nor his donkey, nor anything that is your neighbor's."

Exodus 20:17

Keeping up with the Joneses has become a hobby in the Western world. Many look at their neighbor's modern-day donkey (car) with covetous eyes and then want to buy a new car as soon as possible. If you don't have the money for it, why not take on a loan? Thinking in that way ignores the fact that your neighbor could also have taken on a loan for the car. And for his home improvement. And for his new tv. And that he has a very high debt. Emulate Paul's secret of contentment to prevent yourself from taking on unnecessary credit (Philippians 4:12; Hebrews 13:5).

"Don't buy things you can't afford with money you don't have to impress people you don't like." – Dave Ramsey

3. Borrowing could instill the wrong mindset

We should always keep the key of hard work in our minds as believers

(Proverbs 10:4) to acquire our wealth. A mentality of "it'll be fine" looms when always trusting on the possibility of borrowing. A position of relaxing can then deceive us, but remember: too much of a little sleep, a little slumber is dangerous (Proverbs 6:10-11)! There always comes a time that the loan needs to be paid back.

It could be that for certain businesses or certain strategies borrowing is inevitable. However, if debt can be avoided, we should strive to do so.

Debt is something that can be inherited from parents. Also, the "poverty mindset" can be inherited from parents. Relying on loans could be instilled from your childhood as you saw your parents do the same. You may need to break this stronghold in your mind. Another thing to consider is to check your family background. Are you all struggling with debts and continuing financial insufficiency? There might be a (generational) curse at work. Jesus has given us power to break any curse.

If you are struggling with high debts, which can be very restricting, you may need to stretch your faith and/or change the management of your finances. As debt can be very restricting, you may need to make absolutely sure that you do anything in your might to use Gods promises to improve your financial situation. What do I mean by this? For example, you may need to increase your sowing: *if you sow richly, you will reap richly*. Of course, do all things with wisdom. You may need to check if you steward your finances (the little you may have) correctly. You may need to recheck your overall giving, your walk in excellence, the use of your talents and gifts, your investing possibilities. Of course your prayer life may not be ignored in all of this. If you struggle with debts, let's pray this prayer in faith:

Father God, I come to You in faith. Lord, teach me Your ways and may You show me my faults in wealth management and may You help me to improve. I claim all Your promises concerning the management of my finances. I know that You are my Source. In Your mighty name I come against everything that tries to block my financial well-being, any curse, any demonic force, any mindset problem, I break it all in Jesus' mighty name. I believe that You are able to bring me from a position of debt to a position of favor rapidly. I thank You for all You have done and all You will continue to do, in Jesus' name, amen.

Keep on praying, believing, studying His Word and checking your behavior. If we follow His principles on wealth management, I truly believe that in many cases we can become lenders instead of borrowers;

> *The Lord will open to you His good treasure, the heavens, to give the rain to your land in its season, and to bless all the work of your hand. You shall lend to many nations, but you shall not borrow.*
>
> *Deuteronomy 28:12*

44. Wealth Should Not Blind

Because you say, 'I am rich, have become wealthy, and have need of nothing'—and do not know that you are wretched, miserable, poor, blind, and naked.

Revelation 3:17

In Revelation 3:17, Jesus speaks to a church in Laodicea, a place in ancient Greece. The words are quite shocking, to say the least. The Laodicean church thinks there is no need of anything and everything is going just fine. However, Jesus regards them as *wretched, miserable, poor, blind and naked.* How is it possible that the Laodiceans are not able to see their state of being in the way that Jesus perceives it? *Wealth has blinded them.*

Wealth has blinding capacities. Often it is said that love is blind but I would like to add the love of money makes blind too! While the situation in Revelation 3:17 speaks about a church, I also believe that it can be applied to an individual. You see, in today's society, there is a notion that once you are wealthy you must be doing something good, right?

Public opinion may turn against you if you acquire your wealth through illegal and unethical practices; but otherwise, the acquiring of wealth is generally applauded. Revelation teaches us that a rich church does not automatically mean a good church. In the same way, the richest performer or musician is not automatically the best musician. And is the richest Christian the most righteous Christian? You see how wealth can blind people's judging capabilities?

Guard your heart above all things.

1. Wealth can blind from seeing the road to salvation and form a barrier for being saved.

2. Wealth can blind from giving the right judgment.

3. Wealth can blind from seeing the well-being of others.

4. Wealth can blind from quitting ungodly practices.

All these points speak for themselves, right? It all centers around this way of thinking: "I'm rich, so why should I need God or others" or "I'm rich (and maybe getting richer), so He must be agreeing with my practices, right?"

Guard your heart with all diligence (Proverbs 4:23) to prevent this blindness! Keep on examining yourself (1 Corinthians 11:28) and ask God to examine you as well (Psalm 26:2).

45. Wealth Should Be Monitored Diligently

Be diligent to know the state of your flocks,

attend to your herds;

Proverbs 27:23

The Bible says we should be diligent to know the state of our flocks and we should attend to our herds. In other words, we should monitor our possessions (or wealth) diligently. Why?

For riches do not endure forever, and a crown is not secure for all generations (Proverbs 27:24).

A crown is a symbol of a king. A king sits in a position of honor, glory and splendor. Solomon's advice comes down to: *whatever you possess now will not always last, but will soon be spent, if you do not take care of it diligently.* It is as if Solomon says, even though one can have the wealth of a kingdom, it can soon vanish and no inheritance will be passed through if one does not use knowledge and insight to monitor it.

Solomon's father, King David, had several guards over his great amount of property. Guards over his storehouses, kingly agricultural fields, vineyards, olive trees, fig-trees, flocks, herds, camels, donkeys and treasures (1 Chronicles 27:25-31). Isn't that a great picture of diligently taking care of your wealth and attending to it?

So, do you know the exact amount of money you have in your bank account? Do you know the current value of your house? The current value of your car? Do you own stock but never check its value? Checking these things helps us in enduring our riches and keeping our crown secure. I also believe that when you realize how much you have, this will still the unrest of wanting more and more. In all thy getting get understanding (Proverbs 4:7). I believe monitoring our wealth is profitable to us for the following reasons:

- *It gives you the ability to prepare for possible (investing) opportunities and scenarios as you continually look around and are aware of the current state of affairs*

- *It will prevent you from spending too much and therefore aids in securing wealth.*

- *It will give insight into how much you actually have and this will still your unrest.*

- *It creates gratefulness and joy in your heart.*

Monitoring what we have received from God is also a form of good stewardship. Monitoring our wealth is a key for retaining wealth and passing it on to other generations and is nothing more than counting our blessings. It has been said often, but I really encourage you, brothers and sisters, *count your blessings.*

46. Money Spending is Key in Acquiring and Retaining Wealth

He who loves [only selfish] pleasure will become a poor man;
He who loves and is devoted to wine and [olive] oil will not become
rich.

Proverbs 21:17

The wise store up choice food and olive oil, but fools gulp theirs
down.

Proverbs 21:20

Wise men know that *how* you spend your money is a key in acquiring wealth. We have already covered how giving money to God's Kingdom helps you with the acquiring of wealth but this point is about not spending it lavishly on unneeded things. Wine and olive oil were items associated with lavish feasting and excessive luxury (Proverbs 21:17). If you are a rich person only looking for pleasure *you will become poor (speaks about retaining wealth)* and if you are not rich and keep on spending it on wine and oil you will *not become rich (speaks about acquiring wealth).*

Wise men know how to store up choice food and olive oil (Proverbs 21:20). Realize that Proverbs 21:20 says that both the wise and the foolish have access to the same material but only the wise know how to save up. In other words, the problem is not in the material but *in behavior.*

It's not your salary that makes you rich, it's your spending habits. —*Charles A. Jaffe*

Do you know that a salary raise will not automatically help you out if you experience problems with money? The problems are *behavioral.* If you do not solve your behavioral problems, a salary raise will only increase your spending. From the Bible, we have covered a lot of truths in this book that will definitely transform your spending habits, like:

1. Giving to the Kingdom

2. Practicing contentment

3. Acknowledging the principle of stewardship

There are great tips on changing your spending behavior from the Word. Another great tip which I like and can be derived from the Word of God, is:

The use of an accountability partner;

1 Corinthians 15:33 says: *"Evil company corrupts good habits"* (1 Corinthians 15:33). But it also works the other way around: *good company influences you in having good habits.* Surround yourself with people who

force you to do better. Accountability sounds like a heavy word but it can also be called a discussion partner, support system or something else. I am trying to say that it is already a great first step if you choose somebody available to you, to discuss your money goals with. Don't put your head in the sand when you have money spending problems. If you are married your accountability partner is probably your spouse.

"The habit of saving is itself an education; it fosters every virtue, teaches self-denial, cultivates the sense of order, trains to forethought, and so broadens the mind." —T.T. Munger

I truly believe that the habit of saving is an education itself. There are a gazillion practical tips out on the Internet on how to transform spending and start saving. These are some of my favorite tips:

1. Record your expenses

2. Set savings goals and decide on your priorities

3. Eliminate debt

4. Annualize your spending (25 a week for lunch in the office, sounds a lot more when calculating it as 1.250 a year)

5. Use the 24-Hour Rule. For any non-essential item, wait 24 hours before purchasing to avoid impulsive purchases

6. Take your lunch from home (simple, but it works and saves a lot on an annual basis!)

Of course, when you have reached a position of wealth, spending is also a key in retaining it. A small leak can sink a big ship. Of course, we should not ignore prayer in transforming our spending (habits). As Christians, we should not be ignorant of the enemy's tactics (2 Corinthians 2:11). If we give them the opportunity, demons have the ability to influence our behavior. Are you stuck in a continuing cycle of wrong spending choices and behavior (and/or do you recognize the same pattern in your family members) and it seems like you are always in a position of insufficiency? A curse or demonic interference can be at work.

Let's end in prayer: *Father, I acknowledge that You are the One that gives to me through Your wonderful love. I acknowledge that You have given me a lot and I am content with what I have. I ask that You grant me Your wisdom in my spending habits and in Your name I break and silence any curse or demonic influence working against my finances. Please help me in my weaknesses in behavior and show them to me. May my attention never divert from You and Your Kingdom. May I receive more from You and may I be found a good steward in the end. In Jesus' name, amen.*

47. Wealth Should Be Passed On Through Generations

A good man leaves an inheritance to his children's children, And the wealth of the sinner is laid up for the just.

Proverbs 13:22

I really like the idea of leaving a legacy when I leave this world. A legacy that is so great that even my children's children will benefit from it. I even like the word. *Legacy.* According to the dictionary, a legacy implies:

(1) *Money or property that you receive from someone after they die*

(2) *Something transmitted by or received from an ancestor or predecessor or from the past*

Of course, this "something" that is transmitted should be *something valuable*. First and foremost my heart's desire is to pass on a Godly legacy of strong believers that will impact this planet spiritually. Like in the line of Timothy, his mother and grandmother (2 Timothy 1:5; 2 Timothy 3-14-15) left him a "faith legacy". Something extremely valuable that was a part of their lives.

If the Lord wills, I will also leave a great material inheritance for my children's children. Shouldn't we all aim for this same goal? The Bible says that a good man leaves an inheritance to his children's children. The Hebrew word that is used for inheritance is *nachal* which refers to leaving a *material* inheritance.

> *And Abraham gave all that he had to Isaac.*

> *Genesis 25:5*

Abraham was a good man. He left his inheritance for his son Isaac and even his grandson Jacob benefited from it. Guess what? We are Abraham's sons through faith (Galatians 3:7). The Bible also calls us heirs of God and joint-heirs with Christ. The primary thing here is our spiritual inheritance but it is not merely limited to that. Do you realize what you have access to presently?

> *Now I say that the heir, as long as he is a child, does not differ at all from a slave, though he is master of all,*

> *Galatians 4:1*

Wealth is not only for your own generation but also for the generations to follow. Aim to mature in Christ so you are ready to receive all He has for you. Aim to be that good man or woman who leaves a great inheritance to one's children's children!

"The best thing about money is that it works 24 hours a day and can work for generations." – Robert Kiyosaki

48. Wealth Should Be Distributed To Workers in The Kingdom

Let the elders who rule well be counted worthy of double honor, especially those who labor in the word and doctrine. For the Scripture says, "You shall not muzzle an ox while it treads out the grain," and, "The laborer is worthy of his wages.

1 Timothy 5:17-18

You shall not muzzle an ox while it treads out the grain. Paul quotes this from the law of Moses in the Old Testament. A muzzle is a device that is placed over the mouth and nose of an animal to prevent it from biting or eating. An ox played a crucial role in harvest season and symbolizes a hard worker. The idea that Paul wanted to convey with this metaphor essentially was: a hard worker should not be prevented from eating the fruit of his important labor. Also, *the laborer is worthy of his wages.*

Certainly not every worker in the Kingdom is found on the church's payroll. Consider their case. Remember the rule of proportionality (which was covered in chapter 40)? We are encouraged to give according to the proportion God has prospered us in (1 Corinthians

16:2). If we are prospered a lot by the Lord and do not give to Him and His workers in accordance with our prosperity, I believe we are not doing what we should do. And of course there are (financial) blessings attached to obedience. The more you own, the more is expected from you. This also applies to financial support.

Of course, there are some ministers that use high-pressure tactics to bring in money and who stress finances maybe a little bit too much. On the other hand, there are also many servants of God, that do not even like bringing up the topic of money, fearing that church attendees might frown upon it.

It says a lot that Paul considered it necessary to point out to Timothy (and indirectly the churches he would have to visit) that elders and other laborers deserve to be rewarded financially (1 Timothy 5:17-18). Often it is forgotten how much work apostles, prophets, evangelists, pastors, teachers and other workers put in for the Kingdom (Ephesians 4:11-16).

> *The one who is taught the word [of God] is to share all good things with his teacher [contributing to his spiritual and material support].*
>
> *Galatians 6:6*

> *Remember those who rule over you, who have spoken the word of God to you, whose faith follow, considering the outcome of their conduct.*
>
> *Hebrews 13:7*

Remember the responsibility we have with our wealth. To whom much is given much is required. We are to give the workers in the Kingdom *double* honor (1 Timothy 5:17). This honor is (also) expressed in finances!

49. God Gives Financial Rest

Come to Me, all you who labor and are heavy laden, and I will give you rest.

Matthew 11:28

Matthew 11:28 is a very special verse to me. As we used to use this verse on our church invitation cards for evangelism, it was one of the first verses I memorized as a young believer. I love these words of Jesus: *come to me all you who labor and are heavy laden, and I will give you rest.* It speaks about those that do not have rest because of the sin that presses on their conscience. They labor under the yoke of the law or the burdens of human tradition but do not find rest. All are encouraged to come to Him, lay down their burdens at His feet and look up to Him as personal Savior and Redeemer who can give peace of mind and rest in their souls. Jesus is our ultimate peace giver.

But look at it this way. How many people are nowadays heavy laden with financial burdens? Let's look at the recent statistics (Source: 2019 financial survey of PwC):

- *When asked what causes them the most stress in their lives, more employees say financial matters than those who answer with any other life stressor combined.*

- *65% of women and 52% of men said that financial matters cause them the most stress.*

For couples, money problems cause the most stress on their relationship (36 percent). For younger adults (age 18-54) these problems were almost twice as likely (44 percent to 23 percent) in comparison with older adults (55+). *Source: The Harris Poll (US)*

I believe Jesus' rest is all-inclusive. He promises rest, so this also means *financial* rest. This doesn't mean that He promises to give you millions instantly or to cancel your debt. I am not saying He is not able to, never limit His miracles, but He promises rest. As noted before, money problems are often caused by problems in the inner man (behavioral problems). Do you know the song "Cast your burdens unto Jesus, for He cares for You." Apply this song in your life. A couple of encouraging verses on (financial) troubles:

- *Look at the birds of the air, for they neither sow nor reap nor gather into barns; yet your heavenly Father feeds them. Are you not of more value than they?*

Matthew 6:26

- *Cast your burden on the Lord, And He shall sustain you; He shall never permit the righteous to be moved.*

Psalm 55:22

- *casting all your care upon Him, for He cares for you.*

1 Peter 5:7

- *Peace I leave with you, My peace I give to you; not as the world gives do I give to you. Let not your heart be troubled, neither let it be afraid.*

John 14:27

When I mention financial rest, I am not primarily referring to experiencing rest by having access to a gigantic pile of money so one can lay back in a very comfortable reclining seat. I primarily refer to a peace of mind concerning finances that only God can give. This peace of mind is not connected to the amount available to us on our bank accounts. On the contrary, it is about giving the burden of finances to God knowing that everything will be fine. However, I do believe that wealth in itself also has peace-bringing capacities if handled in accordance with God's plan.

The craving of more and more only God can still. A recent scientific study concluded with "more money, more stress". But remember, wealthy Christians should always be on the winning side: because together with wealth, Christians always should have Christ's peace to go alongside with it.

50. Jesus Was and Is Not Poor

For you know the grace of our Lord Jesus Christ, that though He was rich, yet for your sakes He became poor, that you through His poverty might become rich.

2 Corinthians 8:9

I have heard said "Jesus was poor" or "Jesus was not rich". Is this true? Some have argued that Jesus was poor and that therefore material wealth does not belong to His followers. But was Jesus actually poor? *Absolutely not.*

Let's assume a person has an amount of more than 7 figures available to him in his bank account. However, this person chooses a very simplistic lifestyle and does not use the amount in this bank account. To make it extreme: let's assume the person lives in a tent and does not own any other possessions. Is this person poor? No. It is not so much about *what he has* but *what he has access to.*

Jesus had access to all things (John 16:15), then how could He have been poor? Just because He did not live in a royal palace does not mean He was poor. He had access to an unending food supply (remember the miracle with the loaves and fish) and money was easily available to Him (Matthew 17:27). I am sure someone performing miracles and preaching like Him attracted a lot of financial gifts too, which the Bible also records in Luke 8:3. He even carried a "wallet" (John 12:6). Is this a picture of someone that was empty-handed, needy, in want, that lacked, that was impoverished, underprivileged and unprosperous? No, right? Conclusion: Jesus was certainly not poor.

2 Corinthians 8:9 tells us that He was poor. I believe Him to be poor only at one moment: on the cross. He was stripped of his garments, humiliated and it was the only time He was separated from Father God (Matthew 27:46). I believe the verse could also imply that Jesus was *relatively* poor compared to His position He had in heaven (Philippians 2:6-11). The late Kenneth Hagin also came to the conclusion that Jesus was certainly not poor:

"I believe these scriptural facts are compelling proof that Jesus was not poor, but was a prosperous man. Now I am not suggesting that He lived a lavish or extravagant lifestyle—that would not have been practical for Him. But Jesus had His needs met during His life on earth, and He was able to do what God asked Him to do.

Jesus' prosperity should not surprise us. The Old Covenant promised prosperity to those who walked in the will of God (see Deuteronomy 29:9; Joshua 1:7; 1 Kings 2:3; 1 Chronicles 22:13; 2 Chronicles 20:20 and 26:5; Job 36:11; Nehemiah 1:11, and Psalm 1:1-3)."

It is 100% clear that Jesus perfectly walked in God's will: *"For I came down from heaven, not to do Mine own will, but the will of Him that sent me (John 6:38)."*

Lastly, I want to conclude this point by warning you not to sink into the false belief that we are not allowed to be wealthy by following the false "Poor Jesus Theory". It would be a shame to think we are required to turn down His abundant provision if we want to walk in His ways. Remember, opening your heart is one of the first steps to receive!

Bonus: True Wealth Is In Christ

But what things were gain to me, these I have counted loss for Christ. Yet indeed I also count all things loss for the excellence of the knowledge of Christ Jesus my Lord, for whom I have suffered the loss of all things, and count them as rubbish, that I may gain Christ.

Philippians 3:7-8

You have made it to the end of this book. The last but certainly not least truth: *true wealth is in Christ.*

*Therefore if you have not been faithful in the unrighteous mammon, who will commit to your trust the **true riches**?*

Luke 16:11

Jesus says that if we have not been faithful with money how can true riches be committed to us? What are true riches? With true riches, Jesus means nothing other than *spiritual riches.* Throughout all the biblical truths that this book contains, the following common truth can be discovered: there is nothing inherently wrong with wealth when handled by a pure and sincere Christian heart. In fact, then wealth is a blessing. However, *eternal* spiritual riches should always be placed above *temporary* earthly riches (2 Corinthians 4:18).

> *Or do you despise **the riches of His goodness, forbearance, and longsuffering,** not knowing that the goodness of God leads you to repentance?*

> Romans 2:4

> *To me, who am less than the least of all the saints, this grace was given, that I should preach among the Gentiles **the unsearchable riches of Christ***

> Ephesians 3:8

> *For this reason I bow my knees to the Father of our Lord Jesus Christ, from whom the whole family in heaven and earth is named, that He would grant you, according to the **riches of His glory**, to be strengthened with might through His Spirit in the inner man*

> Ephesians 3:14-16

> *Oh, **the depth of the riches both of the wisdom and knowledge of God!** How unsearchable are His judgments and His ways past finding out!*

> Romans 11:33

Knowing Christ

Like Paul, we should consider knowing Christ more valuable than anything else (Philippians 3:8). Jesus makes it possible for us to have a relation with God the Father through His death on the cross (Romans 5:10).

If you have not yet accepted Jesus, the Person who is true wealth and in whom you can find true wealth, as your personal Lord and Savior, I would like to lead you in accepting Him through prayer. The Bible says in Romans 10:9 that if we confess with our mouth that Jesus is Lord, and believe in our heart that God raised Him from the dead, we will be saved. If you have not yet begun your personal relationship with God, understand that **the One who created you loves you no matter who you are or what you've done.** He wants you to build a strong relationship with Him and you to experience the profound depth of His care.

Tell God that you are willing to trust Him for salvation. You can tell Him in your own words or use this simple prayer:

Lord Jesus, today I give You my heart. I ask You to forgive all of my sins and save me from eternal separation from God. I believe in Your work on the cross and Your resurrection. Thank You for salvation. Thank You for providing the way for me to know You and to have a relationship with my heavenly Father. Through faith in You, I have eternal life. Lord Jesus, I accept You as my personal Lord and Savior. Thank You for hearing my prayers and Your unconditional love. Please come into my heart and give me the strength, wisdom, and determination to walk in the center of Your will from now on. In Jesus' name, amen.

If you have just prayed this prayer, congratulations! You have received Christ as your Savior and have made the best decision you will ever make—one that will change your life forever! Heaven rejoices over you (Luke 15:7).

Ending words

This book is intended to present a whole-sided presentation of God's Word on wealth: great, comprehensive advices to acquire, steward and use wealth properly, as well as warning against dangers in it, plus all the truths on wealth being a blessing for the pure Christian are presented.

Be encouraged to take all the points covered into consideration and my prayer is that you, and therefore ultimately God's Kingdom, will benefit from it.

The truth shall set you free. I want to end with John's words (3 John 2 AMP):

> *Beloved, I pray that in every way you may succeed and prosper and be in good health [physically], just as [I know] your soul prospers [spiritually].*